THE TRAIL TO POVERTY FLAT

FORGOTTEN STORIES OF THE UTAH FRONTIER

DAWN HOUSE

For Paul.
Each day with you is a gift.

Published by TorreyTales: www.torreytales.com

For information or permission, contact the author at: dawn@torreytales.com

Cover image: Ken Baxter, oil on canvas

Editing, design, and publishing services provided by Stephen Carter: steveorstephen@gmail.com.

ISBN: 979-8-9871456-0-9

TABLE OF CONTENTS

LIST OF IMAGES

FOREWORD

All good journalists possess a healthy curiosity. For the best reporters and editors, the big questions of why and how become urgent and passionate quests, even obsessions, to satisfy the need to know and let others in on the story. Throughout her decades of reporting, editing, and teaching, Dawn House has been driven by an intense sense of inquiry.

As an award-winning reporter for *The Salt Lake Tribune*, she broke one of the biggest stories in the so-called Mormon Murders saga when she tracked down 19th-century documents at the center of the LDS Church's doomed business dealings with forger and killer Mark Hofmann. She navigated her way through the secret and byzantine finances of a fundamentalist Mormon polygamous community to reveal systematic abuses of government-provided welfare assistance. More than once during her career, House found herself face-to-face in interviews with religious zealots who would prove to be the most dangerous of men. Bravery is another trait of the best journalists.

Now, House has discovered yet another story to pursue with passion and purpose: The story of a 19th-century home—more accurately described as a shack—she purchased as a weekend getaway to be enjoyed in a well-deserved retirement. The historic structure, in the center of Torrey, Utah, and the gateway to Capitol Reef National Park, sits in one of the most visually stunning locales on Earth. Intending to demolish the small, wood-plank structure and build a modern house, she came to realize that she had purchased a piece of history. For one thing, the walls of her new purchase could, almost literally, speak. Only Dawn House can explain how, but trust me, they do.

She discovered a story with plot strands stretching to the Civil War, the Battle of Little Big Horn, and General George Custer; to the creation of the gravity-defying Hole-in-the-Rock trail that opened southeastern Utah to white settlement and tragic encroachment on native peoples.

Her narrative introduces students of western and Utah history to essential, but previously untold, stories of characters in that infamous chapter of Mormon history, the Mountain Meadows Massacre.

Perhaps House's most important achievement is in revealing how the hard lives of frontier women remain one of history's great, and underreported, stories.

The Trail to Poverty Flat is part history, part memoir, as the author weaves in her own experiences as a journalist, a sister and daughter, and someone who has felt deeply the tragedy of violent encounter. Her brother, Fred House, was a respected and beloved member of Utah's law enforcement community, cut down in the prime of life during a standoff with members of a polygamous sect.

Using all the means in an investigative reporter's toolbox—interviews with descendants, public records, genealogical archives—she merges her own story with that of George and Ethalinda Morrill, the couple who homesteaded Poverty Flat, and in doing so set the foundation for the town of Torrey and Capitol Reef National Park.

Dawn House reminds readers that history lives in us all. And that a tiny frontier dwelling in the southern Utah desert—now lovingly restored—provides an essential thread weaving stories of lives from Utah, and from around the world, connecting then and now.

—TERRY ORME
former editor and publisher of *The Salt Lake Tribune*

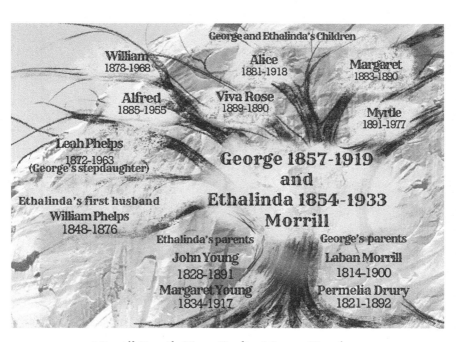

Morrill Family Tree. Credit: Maura Naughton

Morrill Cabin before renovation.
Credit: Ann Torrence

INTRODUCTION

Five days before Christmas in 1886, George and Ethalinda Morrill and their five children moved into a one-room cabin on a windswept bench known as Poverty Flat near today's Capitol Reef National Park. The cabin had no insulation of any kind, no ceiling, and nothing to keep out the frigid winds that blew through the board-and-batten wood plank walls. On Christmas Eve, the children hung their stockings on the south wall's sandstone fireplace.

I stood in that room 130 years later as a recently retired editor and reporter at Utah's largest newspaper, *The Salt Lake Tribune*. I had purchased this weed-infested, half-acre lot in the oldest section of Torrey to build a home. At first, I was just deciding if any materials could be salvaged when I tore the cabin down. But soon, my reporting instincts kicked in and I wondered, "Who built this falling-down shack?" The old house had been boarded up for nearly forty years, clouding memories, but using the investigative tools I relied on during my 35-year newspaper career, I began researching the cabin's history. I found out that it had been built by George Morrill, one of Torrey's founders.

Though I have no ancestral ties to the Morrill family, I started piecing together their stories. I interviewed family descendants and read textbooks, local histories, and 19th-century newspapers. I put together individual family charts, listing the mother, father, children, and grandparents. I included dates of birth, marriages, deaths, and burials to determine places where the family had lived. I also studied

Morrill Cabin interior before renovation.
Credit: Ann Torrence

great-grandparents, nieces, and nephews to get a fuller view of their history. I looked through federal census records for added information, such as home occupants, relatives in the same household, and family members living in the neighborhood. Through these efforts, I learned that the Morrills and their parents were involved in several critical historical events. Their stories just kept tumbling out.

I couldn't bring myself to destroy the last remaining home tied to Torrey's earliest history. My neighbors thought I was crazy to restore the old shack, and I realized they were absolutely correct during many sleepless nights after my money ran out. I was as mad as the proverbial hatter.

I wrote a newspaper story about wanting to restore the cabin and received a surprising telephone call soon afterward from Ken Baxter, a renowned plein (open) air painter. He told me he had stumbled across the cabin's charm years before when he had painted it while on a road trip to Torrey with his wife, Patricia.

Morrill Cabin interior before renovation.
Credit: Ann Torrence

"The cabin was a good subject; it was an interesting place," he said. "The coloration of the wood, its weathering showed it had survived. There was something attractive about it that had withstood the test of time." He thought it embodied the Japanese aesthetic principle Shibui, where beauty is found within rather than without.

He offered to sell the painting to me, but I couldn't afford it. I was bleeding money and didn't have enough equity for a loan. That's when Patricia Baxter stepped in. How much could I offer as a down payment, she asked. Could I pay in monthly installments? She hammered out a meager payment schedule with me, one that would require plenty of patience from them before I could pay it off. It's clear the Baxters wanted me to have the painting. "It belonged in the cabin," said Ken. "Sometimes things work out the way they're supposed to."

When an old friend, who is a real estate agent, viewed the painting, he laughed and said, "Fixing that thing up is going to be a hell of a lot of work."

It was. But it also gave me a surrogate family: the Morrills. Their struggles have resonated with my struggles. The Morrill cabin is the last witness to the town's earliest history and there are too many stories embedded in its walls for me to rightly call myself its owner. In this brief segment of time, I am its caretaker. What follows are the stories I found within its walls and the surprising ways they connected with and enriched my own life.

Dawn House at the Morrill Cabin.
Credit: Leah Hogsten

Restored Morrill Cabin.
Credit: Scott T. Smith

Restored Morrill Cabin interior.
Credit: Scott T. Smith

William Washington Phelps

CHAPTER ONE
Lost Love

"He was an outlaw. I wish I could tell of the beautiful love story she would tell us, all about their courtship. When they were married she knew the kind of life he lived, but she loved him so much she hoped that her love for him in time would change his way of life."

—Cleo Teeples Behunin
Ethalinda's granddaughter

In 1866, William Phelps found himself stranded in Utah.

He traveled a long, bitter road to get there. As a member of the famed Michigan Brigade, he had fought alongside the Union Army in the Battle of the Wilderness in Virginia in 1864—the first clash between Confederate General Robert E. Lee and Union Lt. General Ulysses S. Grant. He was lucky to have survived; the battle claimed 28,700 casualties. He also fought in the Battles of Yellow Tavern (625 dead and injured), Five Forks (2,950 casualties), and Cedar Creek (5,800 casualties). The Michigan Cavalry helped box in Lee, leading to the Confederate surrender at Appomattox Court House. William was one of the 150,000 soldiers who paraded through Washington, D.C., during the victory celebrations.

But that was just the beginning of his journey. The cavalry was downsized and sent by train to Fort Leavenworth, Kansas, where they marched—on foot—to Fort Laramie in present-day Wyoming to battle the Lakota, Sioux, Cheyenne, and Arapaho Indians. This was not a war the soldiers had volunteered to fight. The Michigan governor and congressional delegation protested this extension of the troops' service and lobbied to bring them home, but to no avail. William's commander, James Harvey Kidd, was so incensed that he wrote to his father that if he were a profane man, "I am afraid I would say something that could never be forgiven."[1]

After William fought in the Powder River Campaign in Wyoming, he saw many cavalrymen discharged to go home. His company, however, was rolled into the Michigan First with orders to remain on the frontier. The troops wintered over at Fort Douglas, Utah, situated on a hill above Salt Lake City, its cannons pointed toward the Mormon settlement hostile to the federal government. Here, William Phelps was finally released from duty in March of 1866.

However, Congress delayed travel payments to the discharged troops, leaving many of them, including William, impoverished and abandoned by the Union they had fought so hard to preserve. The soldiers who did make it home arrived destitute and penniless. In Utah, some soldiers took jobs as civilian guards at the Utah Penitentiary; others were appointed to federal offices. The prison warden and the U.S. Marshal both served in the Michigan Brigade, under its famous commander George Armstrong Custer.

William, now in his early twenties, ended up in Kanab in southern Utah. There, he met the headstrong 16-year-old Ethalinda.

Ethalinda Jane Young was born March 27, 1854, in Provo, Utah, situated near the shores of Utah Lake. Her parents called her Janey. With the early death of her brother, Ethalinda became the eldest in the family. She was expected to shoulder the same responsibilities her

---

1. James Harvey Kidd, Letters 1862–1865, 49.

elder brother would have borne. She learned to shoot, was an excellent horsewoman, and could drive a team of horses at an early age.

Provo, settled in 1849, was prosperous, soon to become the second-largest settlement in the Utah Territory after Salt Lake City. Provo townspeople established Brigham Young Academy, the beginnings of Brigham Young University, owned and operated by The Church of Jesus Christ of Latter-day Saints.

Fort Douglas, Utah.
Used by permission, Utah State Historical Society.

Ethalinda's life might have been easier if her parents had remained in Provo, with its abundant streams, fertile valleys, and wildlife. However, the prophet Brigham Young called on her father, John William Young (no relation to Brigham), to build gristmills on the arid frontier. John obeyed, starting a life marked by his family's constant relocation from one outpost to another, either at the command of their prophet or to find a better life.

William and Ethalinda were married on October 23, 1870. The couple followed her parents 160 miles north to Kanosh, where their daughter Leah was born on August 5, 1872.[2]

William's life changed radically when he married Ethalinda. For years, he had camped with hardened veterans with few restrictions imposed by kinfolk, congregations, or communities. In Utah, however, religious rules were strict, and obedience to Mormon leaders was expected.

During a world economic downturn that hit Utah, William fell into the company of outlaws. He drifted from the shelter of an orderly family life to the wild excursions he had been accustomed to in his former days.

In the fall of 1875, William was brought to the Utah Territorial Penitentiary on charges of horse stealing. He quickly formed alliances with other prisoners, some of whom were killers. Four months later, on March 14, 1876, he and six other inmates staged an escape.

The Salt Lake Tribune reported that the breakout had been well planned. The inmates studied the guards' routines and knew their best chance of escape was during the time prisoners were milling around before dinner. In the late afternoon, a prisoner asked Warden Matthew Burgher's permission to fetch some coal for the prison house. As soon as Burgher opened the front gate, several prisoners overpowered him and began beating him with socks filled with fist-sized rocks.

Charlie Williamson, a cattle rustler, grabbed the warden's pistol and kept unarmed guards at bay. Two officers manning rifles atop a stone parapet tried to shoot the escapees but couldn't get a clear shot

---

2. The central town is named for Chief Kanosh, head of the Pahvant band of the Ute Indians, who struggled to ensure the survival of his people through negotiation rather than conflict. In 1929, the federal government granted the tribe official recognition and deeded a small reserve near their ancestral homeland.

without the risk of killing the warden.[3]

When the prisoners couldn't get past the outer gate, they broke into the warden's house. There they beat inmate trustee Harry Gaines until he fell to the floor and played dead. When the warden's housekeeper began screaming, Williamson, the cattle rustler, said they must kill her to stop the noise, but another escapee stopped him. Williamson dragged the housekeeper from room to room until the terrified woman led the prisoners to the front door.

Utah Territorial Penitentiary, 1887.
Used by permission, Utah State Historical Society.

Gaines jumped up from where he had been playing dead, grabbed a Spencer rifle, filled his pockets with cartridges, and gave chase. At a creek, the prisoners split up into two groups, with three running downhill and the other four fleeing in the opposite direction. When

3. Burgher, 35, who served in the same Michigan Cavalry as William, had been seriously wounded at Stone River, one of the war's bloodiest battles. In 2007 the Utah Department of Corrections placed a plaque near Burgher's grave at Fort Douglas in Salt Lake City.

Gaines caught up to the four men, he fired his rifle and ordered them to give up. He marched three men back to the prison at gunpoint and returned to find the fourth man hiding under some bushes. Gaines brought him back and jumped on a prison horse to catch the other runaways, but his mount had been ridden to town twice earlier that day through the mud and could run no more.

William escaped capture and headed south toward the home he shared with Ethalinda. Soaking wet from running across a creek, William knocked on the door of a stranger living in Cottonwood Canyon, a few miles from the prison. He made up a convoluted story about coming into town with some cattle when thieves sneaked up and startled his horse, which reared up and threw him into the creek. He said the robbers ordered him to hand over his vest, coat, and boots, and then for some unknown reason, tossed him one old shoe before galloping away with his cattle.

After listening to William's story, the man gave him a hot supper, a bed for the night, breakfast the following day, a coat, and a pair of rubber boots.

William made his way sixty-five miles south to the home of an escapee's father in Santaquin. The *Deseret Evening News* reported that William knew the old man from prison visits. The man gave him provisions, a Bowie knife, and a pistol. In the morning, William continued south.

Just as the sun was setting, Deputy Sheriff John D. Holladay picked up William's trail. When his posse failed to catch up, Holladay tried to deputize five men riding in a wagon, but they were unarmed and terrified. Mounted on a horse, Holladay, 49, confronted 28-year-old William alone, who was armed but on foot. He ordered William to hold up his hands and was shouting a second time to surrender when William drew his gun, whirled around, and fired at him point-blank. The bullet barely missed Holladay, but the muzzle flash scorched his right hand and cheek.

Holladay fired, hitting William once in the chest. He then leaned over and bashed William on the head, knocking him to the ground.[4] Bystanders carried William to their wagon and transported him to town. Although William claimed he had not assaulted the warden, Holladay put William on a Utah Southern railway car the next day. A doctor aboard gave aid, but William died on the way back to Salt Lake City. The warden died from the fatal beating that same day. The murderers were captured but escaped again and were not apprehended.

Devastated, Ethalinda refused to believe the newspaper accounts. She insisted that William was huddled over a campfire when the deputy sneaked up from behind and shot him in the back. She asked over and over why the deputy hadn't lassoed William and brought him back unharmed.

For the rest of her long life, Ethalinda would maintain a romanticized vision of her slain outlaw husband. In her grief, she initially retreated into the familiar patriarchal society of her birth.

Ethalinda's husband would not rest in peace. In 1951 when the prison was moved from Salt Lake City thirty miles south to Draper, officers forgot where fourteen prisoners had been reburied at the new site. William's remains likely were scattered during construction projects that widened Interstate 15 at Point of the Mountain near the Salt Lake-Utah County border.

Other than Ethalinda, there were few who mourned William, except for a brother.

---

4. The deputy was the son and namesake of John D. Holladay, who had settled a town in Salt Lake County called Holladay, named for the father. Today, Holladay is an affluent city, pop. 31,000, with a country club, golf course, upscale office buildings, and shopping malls.

Lt. Fred House

CHAPTER TWO
Brothers in Arms

When I heard on the news that an officer had been shot, I knew it was Fred. He was the first to volunteer."

—GARY W. DELAND
Utah Corrections executive director
on the 1988 death of my brother Fred House

William Phelps and his older brother Count had a loving, tragically short relationship—much like the bond between my brothers Fred and Tom House. It may have been my love for my brothers, and my memories of how dedicated they were to each other, that led to my intense interest in William and Count. The parallels between their relationships haunted me.

William didn't know much about the comforts of family. Born February 15, 1848, in White Oak, Michigan, the seventh of ten children, he was seven years old when his father, a blacksmith, died. William's mother remarried but was unable to care for her youngest children, so, by 1860, William, who was twelve, and his six-year-old sister, Frances, were boarding in the house of a childless couple.

In February 1864, eleven days before his sixteenth birthday, William lied about his age and joined the military. Being illiterate, he signed his enlistment papers with an "X." His military papers describe him as standing five feet five inches and having gray eyes and light hair. Newspapers later reported he was "a rather large" man, weighing about 180 pounds.

William joined his thirty-one-year-old brother, Count, in the 6th Michigan Cavalry Regiment, led by George Armstrong Custer. Count was the eldest in the family, sixteen years older than William. Count had been so poor when their father died that he could not help his siblings.

Count already had more than two years of combat experience when William joined him. The year before, on July 3, 1863, Count had fought at Gettysburg, Pennsylvania, the costliest battle of the war, with more than 51,000 casualties. His commander wrote that the Michigan men were outnumbered three to one in Custer's charge against the legendary and undefeated J.E.B. Stuart, their sabers raised. "Then it was steel to steel. For minutes—and for minutes that seemed like years— the gray (Confederate) column stood and staggered before the blow: then yielded and fled."[1]

However, before the battle, Count was injured when his unit collided with the Confederate cavalry on the road leading to Gettysburg. A gun barrel hit him in the chest, cracking his ribs. Days later, during the battle at Waterfalls, Maryland, Count's horse stumbled and threw him from his saddle. The fall injured his back and prevented him from riding a horse. His role for the rest of the war was to drive wagons through hostile territory to resupply frontline troops.

William's turn at combat came three months after he enlisted, on May 5, 1864. Alongside the Union Army of the Potomac, William and Count's company fought in the Battle of the Wilderness in Virginia,

---

1. James Harvey Kidd, *Personal Recollections of a Cavalryman with Custer's Michigan Cavalry Brigade in the Civil War*, 152–155.

and the Battles of Yellow Tavern, Five Forks, and Cedar Creek.[2]

Count and William marched triumphantly with the Michigan Cavalry through Washington, D.C., to celebrate the end of the Civil War. A few days later, they said good-bye to each other. William headed on his long route toward Utah, and Count returned to Michigan to rejoin his wife and young son.[3] They would never see each other again.

The story of William Phelps and his brother Count fighting in the same cavalry company reminded me of my own brothers. Fred and Tom were both corrections officers, black belts, and karate teachers in the same Provo, Utah, dojo. But in many ways, they were very different.

Tom, the older of the two, was dark-complected and a couple of inches shorter than his six-foot younger brother. As the warden over the maximum-security section of the state prison,[4] Tom was no-nonsense and precise. He developed policies that withstood legal challenges, such as a smoking ban, conditions warranting the use of force, and grooming standards for both prisoners and guards. Tom told officers the only difference between staff and prisoners was the bars separating them. "The best people have some bad in them, and the worst some good," he often said. Remembering the effects of our father's alcohol-

---

2. Among the casualties was William and Count's brother-in-law Orrin Bentley, who was twenty-six. He was wounded and taken prisoner on May 6, 1864. He died two months later in a prisoner-of-war camp in Richmond, leaving behind a wife and two young sons. The Phelps's 20-year-old brother, Henry, died on Oct. 21, 1864, as Union forces cut railway lines in Virginia. He was killed 10 months after enlisting in the Fifth Michigan Infantry Regiment, nicknamed the Fighting Fifth, which suffered some of the highest casualty rates in the Union army.

3. There he became a farmer, despite his painful back and chest injuries, and fathered three daughters. The name of his company and regiment are emblazoned on his tombstone.

4. Tom retired in 2019 as an auditor for the Utah Department of Corrections.

ism, Tom did not drink. He was calm, professional, and never used profanity.

On the other hand, Fred was freewheeling. One of his first acts as a student at the Mormon-owned Brigham Young University was to drop a religion class taught by a fundamentalist instructor. The irate instructor asked Fred if he lacked the courage, integrity, and faith to finish the course. "Yup," Fred replied. "That about sums it up."

Fred was a lieutenant on the prison SWAT team and head of the Canine Unit. He looked for parole violators and runaways, often apprehending the highest number of escapees. Whenever he captured a suspect late at night, he would call his boss at home and sing an off-key song popularized by The Bobby Fuller Four: "I fought the law, and the law won."

He was always willing to help, and thus had a lot of friends. One night, Fred heard on the radio that Salt Lake City officers were clearing out a drug house. So, on his way home, though suffering from a cold, he stepped in with his dog to make sure no suspects were hiding inside. He also helped several departments set up their own canine units.

The night of January 16, 1988, the Singer-Swapp clan (a polygamist group) bombed a Mormon chapel in Marion, Utah, a farming town about fifty miles east of Salt Lake City, and fled to their compound that sheltered nine adults and six children. It didn't take long for the authorities to zero in on the Singer-Swapps, who were known for their hatred of the Mormon Church and the government. Indeed, Swapp said later that the bombing was revenge for the 1979 police slaying of polygamist patriarch John Singer in a standoff. He believed an armed confrontation would resurrect Singer.

The FBI surrounded the compound, beginning an armed standoff. Agents who had worked with Fred asked him to join them in capturing the perpetrators. On the thirteenth day of the standoff, January 28,

1988, Fred helped execute a plan that officers hoped would subdue Adam Swapp, the ringleader, who was holed up in a nearby barn where he had gone to milk the goats.

As Fred attempted to unleash his dog, Timothy Singer, hidden in the compound's shadows, shot Fred with a rifle. The bullet smashed through the ceramic plate of his bullet-proof vest, and Fred dropped.

Immediately, FBI agents fired two rounds, wounding Swapp, who quickly surrendered. But gunfire burst out as agents moved in an armored personnel carrier to evacuate my brother's body. The clan fired more than one hundred rounds from their hiding places in the log house, hitting two other officers.

As one member of the medical team wrote later, "When Fred was hit, myself and another medic worked on him for a long time, but there was nothing we could do to save him. Believe me, we tried. [I] know that Fred loved what he was doing and would have done it again if he had been asked."[5]

My brother Tom identified Fred's body and took on the role of protecting his brother's family. When an insurance company denied benefits to Fred's widow, Ann, Tom proved the company's claim was bogus and threatened to go public with their refusal to pay benefits. Ann received the money.[6]

The task of going through Fred's personal effects also fell to Tom. He retrieved a scale Fred had brought home from a drug raid, which

---

5. Swapp, his mother-in-law (Vicki Singer), and her sons Timothy and Jonathan were convicted of multiple charges in state and federal court. None drew more prison time for their roles in my brother's death than for conspiring to bomb the empty chapel. All four have since been released from prison.

6. Ann and I grew closer after Fred's death. She has become an inspiration to families whose loved ones were killed in the line of duty. She has consistently refused to be defined by Fred's death or the perpetrators who killed him. Even now, decades later, Ann receives invitations to speak.

he had used to weigh miniature cars for the pinewood derby race his 8-year-old son had participated in at church days before Fred's death.

Tom gave the eulogy at the funeral, held on Fred's 36th birthday. At the graveside, my brothers' Shotokan Karate master, Tsutomu Ohshima, summoned a lifetime of perfecting the inner power of Chi to speak to Fred, saying, "You accomplished life beautifully."

Those words are etched on Fred's tombstone.

Six months after Fred's death, a corrections training building was named the Fred House Academy Training Center. Once, when I stopped to do an interview at the FBI offices in Salt Lake City, I saw Fred's portrait hanging on the wall.

I was working at *The Salt Lake Tribune* the morning of Fred's death. My colleagues urged me to go home, but I put my anguish aside, knowing Fred would have expected me to write his story. As the *Chicago Tribune* put it:

Nowhere was the grief surrounding the now-ended 13-day standoff at the Wasatch Mountain compound of a polygamy cult more wrenching than on the front page of Friday's *Salt Lake Tribune*.

There, in a black box, was staff writer Dawn Tracy's[7] obituary for her 35-year-old brother, Freddie Floyd House, a Utah prisons department officer killed in the gunfire that ended with the cult's surrender in the compound 60 miles northeast of here. ...

In the obituary, Tracy recalled that her brother, a slender and mustachioed karate expert who left three young children, "couldn't walk without swaggering. Officers at the prison said he was the last man they'd want around when they needed a diplomat and the first in a riot. "We called him Marshal Dillon..."

---

7. For my byline, I used my married name, Tracy—which I changed to House, my maiden name, after my divorce.

"I didn't want anyone else to write Fred's story," she ended. "He was my brother. He was my dear, old friend."

George Drury Morrill

CHAPTER THREE
The Scout Who Rode Away

"The time will come when you shall see the benefit of your labors which, at the present time, is not known among thy neighbors."

—A Mormon rite, or blessing,
given to frontier scout
George Morrill in 1912,
six years before his death.

George Morrill, who would eventually marry the widow Ethalinda, was known as a founder of Torrey, Utah. But his real fame rests on his scouting exploits in the Hole-in-the-Rock Expedition.

In the 1870s, the power of Mormon prophet and colonizer Brigham Young extended beyond Utah to Nevada, a large portion of Arizona, about one-third of California and Colorado, and parts of New Mexico, Wyoming, Oregon, and Idaho. He had envisioned settlements abutting Monument Valley, located in lands sacred to the Navajo Nation. In 1879, Young's successor, John Taylor, called on some 250 men, women, and children to leave their homes in southern Utah to colonize the far eastern side of the Territory. It was called the Hole-in-the-Rock trek—one of the nation's most famous and treacherous road-building expeditions.

Settlers living in southern Utah, where most families in the expedition came from, were among the poorest of the Saints. About 200 miles to the north, the average value of an acre of land in Salt Lake County was $75, compared to $34 and $9, respectively, in Washington and Iron counties, according to an 1870 U.S. farm report.[1] Mormon leaders issued directives to the faithful living in these two counties to sell their homes and move east to the San Juan settlement—at their own expense.

In the fall of 1879, the trek began in the town of Escalante and went through today's Grand Staircase-Escalante National Monument. The Hole-in-the-Rock Expedition was only 250 miles, compared to the 1,300-mile trail the Mormons had travelled from Illinois to Salt Lake City, but it took these settlers twice as long to break through the redrock wilderness. Wagon leader Jens Nielson had lost his five-year-old son while pulling a handcart to Salt Lake Valley in 1859 and was adamant that the settlers continue their journey into the unknown wilderness.[2] The expedition was tasked with joining a small, struggling colony established the previous year at Montezuma Creek near the Utah/Arizona border. The settlements would act as a buffer against outlaws, American Indians, and non-Mormon settlers (dubbed gentiles).

The pioneers hoped to find a shortcut, which could cut 500 miles from the journey to Montezuma Creek, situated near the turbulent San Juan River. Each day, the wagon train had to pick its way across lands that became wilder, slowing the trek to a standstill. The mile-long train of 83 wagons and 1,000 head of cattle had already set out when they received word from an advance exploring party that finding a shortcut was downright impossible.

---

1. Rainfall is key to the disparity in wealth between Utah's northern and southern counties. Salt Lake Valley and surrounding areas enjoyed as much as three times the precipitation, enough to support tidy farms and prosperous ranches. Precipitation is fifteen inches, compared to five to ten inches in the south.

2. Cornelia Adams Perkins, *Saga of San Juan*, 319–320.

The region's scenic wonders would inspire future novelists and film directors, but settlers saw little of its beauty as they struggled to get their wagons through the badlands. Expedition leader Platte Lyman described the rough, redrock terrain in his journal: "The country here is almost entirely solid sand, rock, high hills and mountains cut all to pieces by deep gulches which are in many places altogether impassable."[3] But, as historian David E. Miller wrote, "This was really easy terrain to cross compared to what lay ahead."[4]

The pioneers were finally forced to stop at what they called Hole-in-the-Rock, a steep, narrow crevice cascading down a towering mountain that looked impassable. At a place they called Fifty Mile Spring, the settlers had little water, scarce fuel for cooking, and no grasses for their livestock. No one in the company had traveled to the area—or knew anyone who had. Yet after discussions and prayers, the pioneers opted to push ahead, leaving themselves at the mercy of winter snows and blizzards if they could not find a way out on the other side of the river.

The wagon master picked four men to find a path to the Montezuma settlement, some seventy miles straight east. The 22-year-old George Morrill was the youngest man selected for this critical mission. The 47-year-old George Sevy was the second-ranking captain in the wagon train. Lemuel H. Redd Sr., 43, had accompanied his son and daughter-in-law on the trek. George Hobbs was a 23-year-old bachelor who helped settle the Montezuma outpost months earlier. He alone could recognize landmarks near the hamlet, and he alone would record their experiences.

On December 17, 1879, the scouts painstakingly picked their way from the top of the Hole down to the Colorado River. They travelled light with two horses, two mules packing their bedding, and a few days of provisions.

---

3. Allen Kent Powell, *San Juan Country, Utah: Resources and History*, 101.

4. David E. Miller, *Hole-In-The-Rock: An Epic in the Colonization of the Great American West*, 71.

Hole-in-the-Rock
Credit: G. Thomas/Wikimedia Commons

The scouts crossed the river and soon came to a place where a previous scouting party had turned back because they could not find a way down a steep, slick rock mountain. But Hobbs spotted mountain sheep on what today is called Lookout Rocks and followed a steep, smooth slope that wound its way to the bottom. They headed east to what was later called Lake Pagahrit, a natural dam created by shifting sand dunes with no grasses or foliage.

The men pressed on until they came to the entrances of three canyons. Not knowing which way to go, they split up. George Morrill and Lemuel Redd explored the northeast fork after deciding it might be an open canyon because it was a little larger than the other two. Their instincts were correct. The south and southeast canyons dead-ended after about a mile of hard climbing.

On the third day, the men came upon an ancient cliff dwelling. They discovered seven rooms and an oven that looked like it could bake bread if the scouts cleared away the debris. The Cliff People lived in the region from about 200 to 1300 A.D., but abruptly left, leaving behind sturdy stone and earth dwellings, exquisite pottery, and scattered trails. Navajos named these people the Anasazi or "Ancient Ones." Archeologists call them Ancestral Puebloans. Sometimes, it's said, winds blowing through the mountains carry faint strains of a long-ago song.

The scouts couldn't find a path below the cliff dwelling, but they followed a wash for several miles until they came upon another ancient trail. They followed the path, which Hobbs described as "well defined and plain in most places," leading them to a break in the surrounding cliffs. The men were forced to stop at Grand Gulch, a formation boxed in by perpendicular walls standing as high as 2,000 feet. They found broken remnants of a path and followed it as best they could. On the sixth day out, they camped and set free their horses and mules to forage. But heavy snows began falling, which soon covered the trail, obliterating the animals' tracks. The men spent critical time looking for them before they resumed their journey through fierce storms and freezing temperatures.

On December 25, the men ran out of supplies. "It was Christmas Day, 1879, which found us on the side of Elk Mountains without food in the midst of a piercing cold, and not a mountain in sight that I could recognize," Hobbs remembered. "I was the only member of the party that had been in Ft. Montezuma on a previous trip. It surely looked like our bones would bleach not far from that point, as it was impossible for us to retrace our steps to our river camp and not knowing which way to go to reach our destination on the San Juan."

George Morrill wrote years later how he coped with despair: "I arose early and knelt in prayer and asked the blessing of the Lord upon me that I may faithfully perform my mission and prove faithful."

Discouraged and weak from hunger, Hobbs made his way to a knoll. And there in the distance he finally saw what he knew to be the Blue Mountains. After more than a week of exploring, it was the first landmark he recognized. The formation was named Salvation Knoll; it stands near today's Natural Bridges National Monument.

However, the Blue Mountains were about ten miles away, putting the men in danger of starving before they could reach their destination. They camped that night in still another cliff dwelling. "This was an eventful Christmas for us poor men," Hobbs remembered. "No food but yet hopeful."

The next day the scouts came to a break in a cliff where Hobbs said the Anasazi "had previously done a vast amount of work in making a trail leading up the side to the top." The men made some repairs and pushed and pulled their livestock to the top of the ridgeline. Hobbs carved his name and date on a rock, "not knowing that I would survive the journey."

In the morning, the men narrowly missed passing Navajos, which was fortunate. Fifteen years earlier, the U.S government had expelled the Navajo from their ancestral lands in what is now Arizona. The genocidal war brought about the Long Walk, which entailed more than fifty forced marches at gunpoint. Many Navajos died of exposure and starvation during the frigid winter resettlements. The Navajo never forgot the outrages against their people.

The scouts searched for their horses and mules, fearing the Navajos had rounded them up. But they found them in a secluded canyon and pushed them down into a wash. Hobbs said if an animal had been killed in the slide, the famished men would have eaten the carcass, which could have sickened or killed them.

On the fourth day, the weary men slogged through slush and mud nearly up to their knees before coming to a valley. They struggled through the muck until they arrived at an isolated homestead on the

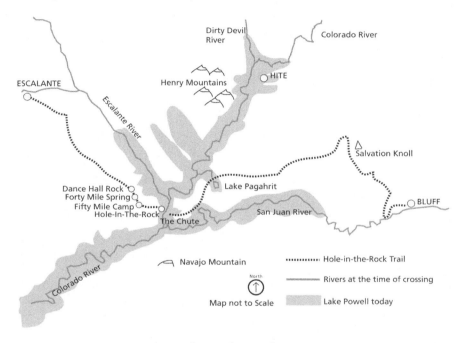

Hole-in-the-Rock expedition map.
Credit: National Parks Service

present site of Bluff, near the San Juan River. The family offered them a bite of meat and some biscuits. Hobbs confessed that he recklessly gobbled down twenty-two biscuits. He didn't care about the risk in his weakened state, saying, "I thought this would be a happy death."

Despite their exhaustion, the scouts hiked twenty miles upstream to Fort Montezuma, where the struggling settlers had nothing more to offer than wheat seeds ground up in a coffee mill. It was a diet the settlers had been subsisting on for the past two months. The scouts dared not eat more. The seeds were needed to plant crops in the spring.

The scouts met a passing trapper who sold them forty-eight pounds of flour for twenty dollars. It was the only food they could get for the return trip to the main camp. They had traveled twelve days to find a passageway to the San Juan River and blizzards slowed their journey back. Their horses' hoofs were severely worn, leaving bloody prints in the snow. But the men were so weak they continued taking turns riding the suffering animals. Their flour gave out three days before they reached the base camp. When they came to the backbone between the San Juan and Colorado Rivers, a lookout from the wagon train waved them down. Ahead, men carving out a trail shared their rations.

The scouting party rejoined the wagon train at the Hole, having been gone twenty-four days instead of what they believed would be eight. They saw that Mormon converts from Wales, familiar with dynamite, had blasted through the rock. The pioneers widened the crevice just enough for their teams and wagons to pass down the steep decline, using pulleys and board walkways to get their wagons through the Hole. On the other side of the river, they were building roads all the way to the San Juan settlement. No one had died. In fact, two babies had been born.

As soon as George Morrill rejoined the wagon train, he left the seventy families whose lives he helped save. Sevy stayed on to build roads and cut dugways to the San Juan River. Redd rejoined his family after helping his son and daughter-in-law make it to the settlement. Sevy and Redd eventually joined Mormon colonies in Mexico to escape federal marshals cracking down on polygamists. Hobbs settled in Juab County, which, fed by mighty streams from the Wasatch Mountains, was prosperous. His wife, Julia, gave birth to eleven children, including triplets and two sets of twins.

Hobbs criticized his old comrades, all three dead by that time, when he was interviewed in 1919 for the LDS Church publication *Deseret Semi-Weekly News*. He insisted that the three other scouts constantly complained, or "murmured," wanting to turn back or run away, while he alone kept pushing ahead. But it's preposterous that any of the men would abandon their families. Two of the scouts had loved ones back at the Hole, and George had to know that people would die if the wagon train became trapped in the winter snows.

It's likely Hobbs confused the story of his companions with Nephi's story in the faithfuls' sacred Book of Mormon where an ancient family flees the destruction of Jerusalem. In Hobbs' account, the three scouts supposedly complained, just like two of Nephi's brothers, who "murmured" about their plight and wanted to turn back when they encountered difficulties. Hobbs spent his remaining years in Nephi, the namesake town for the Book of Mormon leader, dying there in 1921 at the age of sixty-four.

The Hole-in-the-Rock Expedition inspired the 1950 movie *Wagon Master*, directed by John Ford. The plot centers around Mormon settlers, joined by a medicine show troupe, journeying through a wilderness to southeastern Utah. The famed athlete Jim Thorpe, a Sac and Fox Nation member, appeared in the movie as a Navajo. The film, considered a masterpiece, followed a classic Ford theme: a community in the West surviving through cooperation for the common good.

Ethalinda was unaware of her husband's heroism in the Hole-in-the-Rock Expedition.[5] In her old age, she told a granddaughter about George leaving her alone with two babies but she did not know any other information. More than a century later, descendants submitted his biography to the Fort Bluff Historic Site. The settlers hadn't forgotten George Morrill, but they only remembered his name.

---

5. George talked little about himself or shared personal feelings, even in his private journals. When he wrote about meeting the Mormon prophet after a lifetime of service, he only recorded the date.

CHAPTER FOUR
Healing Powers of the Navajo

"If my work does nothing else when I get to the end of my life, I want Native peoples to be seen as human beings."

—JOY HARJO
the nation's first Native American poet laureate,
a Muscogee Nation member

The Hole-in-the-Rock Expedition represented a hard-won victory for the Mormon settlers. Stories of the trek mention that paths built by ancient Native Americans were key to its success. Sadly, the expedition, which brought throngs of white settlers into the previously isolated region, had wide-ranging consequences for the Navajo people who had populated southern Utah for centuries.

The whites dominated politics in the area for 135 years until, in 2016, a Utah federal judge ruled that voting maps in San Juan County were unconstitutional. Even though Navajo voters make up more than half the county's population, they were packed into one of three districts. The racially gerrymandered voting districts guaranteed that no more than one Navajo could serve on the three-member commission. Seats on the school board were even more skewed.

Navajo elder Willie Grayeyes was singled out in the push to maintain white power. Grayeyes helped put together a coalition of tribes to win federal protections for Bears Ears National Monument. Named for a pair of massive buttes that stand out against spectacular scenery, it is considered sacred land for many Native Americans, containing thousands of years of rock art, cliff dwellings, and other ancient artifacts. But the white-held county majority bitterly opposed the designation.

After Grayeyes announced his candidacy, San Juan County officials removed his name from the county commission ballot, questioning his qualifications. A federal judge, however, reversed the decision, citing altered documents by those county officials to justify their claims.

The county commissioners did not give up. They claimed Grayeyes did not live in the county and tried once again to strike his name from the ballot. But Greyeyes insisted that his home at Paiute Mesa near the Arizona line was on the Utah side of the Navajo Reservation. (Navajo lands also stretch into Arizona and New Mexico.) Records showed that Grayeyes had voted in San Juan elections for the past twenty years.

The U.S. 10th Circuit Court of Appeals upheld the newly drawn voting districts. After the ruling, a first-ever majority Navajo commission was elected, including Grayeyes.[1]

In 2017, then President Trump shrunk the size of Bears Ears by a whopping eighty-five percent. The 1.35-million-acre site was cut into two smaller, noncontiguous units that were opened for mining, development, and mechanized vehicles. This time, the new commission challenged Trump's downsizing, with Greyeyes casting the deciding vote. In 2021, President Biden restored full protections to Bears Ears

---

1. In 2022, Republicans took back control of the San Juan County Commission after residents voted out the first Native American majority for any county commission ever elected in Utah. Democrats Grayeyes and Kenneth Maryboy lost their reelection bids. The two Navajo members were the target of corruption allegations. Opponents had pressed Utah Attorney General Sean Reyes, an election denier, to investigate them during the election season.

Willie Greyeyes

and the Grand Staircase-Escalante National Monument, where most of the Hole-in-the-Rock trail is located.

In San Juan County, power brokers have discussed splitting the county, giving whites and Navajos their own jurisdictions. However, most of the resources, such as critical infrastructures and schools, would be on the side where whites live.

Grayeyes also has supported building a road to Navajo Mountain to connect the area's five hundred residents to Utah's highway system. Currently, residents must drive through Arizona to haul drinking water and groceries to their homes. The community center at Navajo Mountain is only forty-five miles from Monument Valley, where a health clinic is located, but it requires a 120-mile drive to get there.

"I encourage anyone who has never been to Navajo Mountain to drive on the existing road," Grayeyes told me in an interview. "They'll understand its extreme isolation and remoteness."

I will admit that my sympathies lie with the Navajo, because of my father, Stan House.

My father was not like most men of his time, perhaps because he was reared by a single working mother. He rejected 1950s norms that confined women to the home. He told me I could do anything, including driving his big rig, even when my feet couldn't reach the pedals. Dad was muscular from offloading cargo. He loved showing off his athleticism on the schoolyard gym rings.

Dad's trucker buddies were my first mentors. They often dropped by our home to drink beer on the patio. We lived in the Los Angeles suburb of Azusa, one of a few California towns with a Native American place name—a fact not taught in my school.

Virtually all of Dad's friends were uneducated, but they usually discussed world events because of their military service. I was hungry to learn about their experiences, so they introduced me into their world of politics and history. I remember one man, a Cherokee, explaining the Trail of Tears.

President Andrew Jackson signed the Indian Removal Act into law in 1830. In 1831, the U.S. military began marching Native Americans living in the southeastern states to present-day Oklahoma. Among those who walked the 5,000-mile trail were Cherokee and Muscogee allies who helped Jackson win the 1815 Battle of New Orleans. By 1850 some 60,000 people were forcibly removed. No one bothered to keep numbers, but it's estimated that at least 4,000 people died from extreme exposure, disease, and starvation. My father's buddy said his people refused to carry a $20 bill because Jackson's portrait is on its face.

I also learned that, despite being forced from their homeland, the Choctaws helped the U.S. during World War I by sending coded radio messages using their language; the enemy never succeeded in deciphering them.[2] In recognition of all Native Americans' military service, they were granted citizenship in 1924.

But racism still runs strong in our country. A woman accosted a Ute friend of mine at a grocery store, telling him to go back to his country—ignorant that her own ancestors are America's latecomers. His neighbors thought they were funny when they nicknamed him Chief. When his mother passed, he reported her death to the Bureau of Indian Affairs. When the agent briefly left his office, he told a colleague he had to handle the case of "some dead Indian."

During World War II, my dad lied about his age to be accepted into the U.S. Coast Guard and was sent to the South Pacific. He helped save his friend Bill after their troop ship went down during a cyclone. Bill had panicked, but Dad stayed with him and helped him swim to shore. When Bill met us in California, he pulled me aside and said, "Your Dad really did save my life." Dad didn't talk about the storm but joked about how Bill Shepherd's family couldn't feed him enough when he visited Bill's home in Florida.

Dad had a penchant for helping people. He delivered dairy products to the Marine Corps Air Ground Combat Center at Twentynine Palms and sometimes picked up Marine hitchhikers going AWOL. On the drive, Dad would help them think their decision through, and whenever he could persuade one to change his mind, he would backtrack to the base and drop them off.

In the days before police took domestic violence seriously, a woman living across the street would run to our house to escape her husband when he beat her. She was in ill health, timid, and walked with a limp.

---

2. Many decades later, I drove a washboard road to Navajo Mountain. I asked a Navajo representative if he would direct me to an elderly Code Talker, who served during World War II. The representative explained that I would need a guide to locate the veteran, and even then, "I'm not sure we could find him."

Dad would step out onto the driveway to calm down the husband until police officers arrived. The man never confronted our father, even though he could see his wife peering through our front door. He may have been intimidated by Dad's many tattoos when only sailors and truck drivers decorated their bodies in ink. Dad was both.

The police would only scold the man and send him home to sleep off the alcohol—until the next drunken rage. My siblings and I saw it all. Every time. My brothers Fred and Tom House may have gone into law enforcement because they saw our father protect this abused woman who had nowhere else to hide.

But Dad could be wild. He sometimes came home bruised from a nasty bar fight. He deeply regretted dropping out of junior high school. And his absentee father disrespected him while praising himself for paying our light bills. Dad couldn't handle money and constantly fought with my mother over finances and his drinking.

My father's personal contradictions were manifest one Christmas Eve when my brothers and I piled into our car to pick up our grandmother. She was babysitting our four cousins during the holiday. When Dad learned that their father was out partying and there were no presents under the tree, we drove around until he found a store still open. He spent all his cash buying gifts, wrapping paper, scotch tape, ribbons, and candy to fulfill the Santa role for his brother's children. We barely had enough gas to get home.

The hero we saw in him that night was tempered when a cop stopped him for weaving on the road. He lectured Dad about driving with an open container of alcohol and waved us on our way.

When he was thirty-eight years old, Dad was boating with his buddies off the coast of southern California when one of the men jumped into the ocean for a swim. The waves became choppy, and he yelled for help. My father was a great swimmer and confidently dove in without a life jacket. A passing trawler picked up his friend, but my father's body went missing for ten days. It was hellish not knowing his fate, which became a recurring nightmare. Adding to my misery, I had fought with my father the last time I had seen him. I was rebellious and angry about his heavy drinking. For years, I had reoccurring nightmares that I had found Dad, who was dying on a beach. He told me the fight we had before his death didn't matter, but I did not believe my dreams.

After his death, the only detail I could remember about the man Dad saved was that he was a Native American. Years later, when Norman Begay, one of my brothers' Navajo friends, heard the story, he and some other members of the Navajo Nation honored our father by giving us an exquisite rug for what, they said, he had done "for our brother."

This first-ever recognition of my father was intensely healing and put to rest the final chapter of his life for me. Each time I open the door to the cabin that George Morrill built, I see the rust-and-gold, hand-knotted rug, and I think of my father and the kindness of a people who were pushed aside in a rush to steal their lands and culture.

Ethalinda Phelps Morrill

CHAPTER FIVE
A Divided Heart

"Say not the Father hath not heard your prayer. You shall have your desire, sometime, somewhere."

—"Unanswered Yet"
sung at Ethalinda's funeral

Ethalinda was still grieving the loss of her first husband, William Phelps, when she moved with her parents to the central Utah town of Circleville. To ease her grief, her father gave her a spirited bay mare named Flo. Townspeople often saw the beautiful, petite woman taking wild rides, her long skirts and auburn tresses flying in the wind.

William's death left Ethalinda and their three-year-old daughter in poverty. Ethalinda worked at a dairy where she milked twenty cows twice each day, churned butter, and did heavy farm chores. She became so bone-weary that she worried no one would care for her child should she die.

Ethalinda's attachment to her daughter did not deter her many suitors. She was desperate, to be sure, but she was hoping for the kind of romance she had shared with her first husband. But the hardworking and pious George Morrill somehow won her over. In 1877, the Morrills were married in the St. George Temple, where only the faithful may enter. The couple and Ethalinda's daughter, Leah, were sealed in sacred rites that Mormons believe would keep them together for eternity.

In her wedding portrait, Ethalinda's personality is on full display. Unlike many women who wore their hair in a severe bun, her curls are unbound, cascading down her shoulders. Ethalinda, 23, looks directly at the camera, bold, self-assured, and confident of her womanhood.

George's tintype shows a serious, handsome man with a determined, piercing gaze. George, 21, would never take a plural wife when it was believed that a woman risked eternal damnation if she did not accept her husband's decision to enter into polygamous marriages.

Ethalinda and George settled into the common lifestyle of the day. They often relocated, sometimes for a better life, and sometimes at the behest of their church leaders—making their lives not much different from that of their parents'. Ethalinda gave birth to George William in Johnson Fort, Iron County, in 1878. The family called him William, after her first husband and her father. Thirty months later, the fiery Alice was born in Junction, Piute County.

The Morrills followed Ethalinda's parents to Loa, about sixty-five miles southeast of Circleville, where George's father-in-law, John William Young, built a gristmill. Two more Morrill children were born in Loa: Margaret in 1883 and the shy Alfred in 1886. George and his father-in-law bought water shares from a local rancher twenty miles southeast of Loa and built two homes for their families on a bench nicknamed Poverty Flat.

George had little schooling, but he had a poet's imagination. In 1886, he located his cabin directly south of what would be called Torrey Knoll, which stood at the foot of the towering Thousand Lake Mountain. The view of the redrock, 100-story knoll would fill the north window, creating a scenic illusion of a master painting.

But George Morrill was too poor to buy logs from the local sawmill. Instead, he purchased wood planks. He drove four cornerstones deep into the rocky soil and built floor joists between the sandstone piers. He stacked vertical planks for the walls and nailed each seam with half-inch strips of wood, called board-and-batten construction.

Five days before Christmas, the couple moved into the one-room cabin, along with eight-month-old Alfred, their four other children, and Ethalinda's daughter, Leah. The Morrills' eldest son, William, remembered trapping rabbits as an 8-year-old boy to keep the family in meat the first winter.

One of their daughters remembered that on Christmas mornings, stockings were filled with a polished apple, a bit of hard candy, and peanuts. Sometimes Ethalinda placed a tin cup, whistle, or trinket in the bottom of their stockings. The cabin, even when enlarged, was never big enough for a Christmas tree.

The day before Christmas, Ethalinda rendered lard for mince pies. She also stirred up a pan full of twists or fried cakes, made from sweetened dough, cut into strips, and fried. She may have followed popular recipes that were published in newspapers of the time:

Mince Meat Pie

Two pounds of beef chopped fine, after being cooked; two pounds of suet, chopped fine; four pounds of raisins; four pounds of apples; eight oranges; the peel of half a pound of citron all chopped fine; one ounce of cinnamon, one of allspice, one of nutmeg and two pounds of brown sugar. (*Salt Lake Herald-Republican*, 1890)

Old Fashioned Fried Cakes

Take 1 cup sugar, 1/2 cup shortening, one pint sour milk and teaspoonful saleratus (sodium bicarbonate), season with allspice or nutmeg, mix with sufficient flour, but not too hard. Have your lard hot enough to make the cakes a darkish brown. These cakes can be made very quickly and will keep a long time in cool weather and do not get stale or dry. (*Woman's Exponent*, 1876)

The family was poor, so meals were simple. Fresh fruit during winters would not be available until the early 1900s when Ethalinda finally could afford canning bottles. Ethalinda could get by with ten pounds of sugar each year, while molasses was a longtime staple. The family had milk and eggs as long as they were not needed to trade for other necessities. Dinners usually consisted of pork, potatoes, onions, and boiled cornmeal mush, sweetened with molasses. Sometimes the cornmeal was fried as a Johnny cake:

Johnny Cake

Take one pint of milk, one pint of meal, three tablespoonfuls of flour, two tablespoonfuls of sugar, one tablespoonful of butter and add one egg. (*Salt Lake Herald-Republican*, 1879)

In the spring of 1887, George Morrill and his father-in-law began plotting canals and streets, using the North Star as a guide. The men aspired to a goal larger than themselves. Their efforts would not conclude with a single, isolated ranch on the lands located near today's Capitol Reef National Park. They would build a community.

It took years for the Morrills' orchard to bear fruit, so the children picked wild berries along Sand Creek for jam preserves. Ethalinda planted carrots, onions, shallots, and squash. She harvested garden sage, which she sold or bartered for goods. She also planted golden willow trees near the dirt street. She placed a barrel underneath the willows to keep water softened with wood ashes. Ethalinda used the clean water to wash clothes when rainstorms muddied the creek. Despite her efforts, clothing was often tinted red from the creek water.

Early years in Poverty Flat were difficult and heartbreaking. In

1890, a diphtheria epidemic struck the tiny village, likely from contaminated drinking water hauled from the creek and open ditches. Seven-year-old Margaret died of the infectious disease, as did their six-month-old baby, Viva Rose, who succumbed three days later.

That same year, Leah, Ethalinda's daughter with William Phelps, ran away the day before her eighteenth birthday to marry Walter Lee.[1] Ethalinda was heartbroken to be excluded from her daughter's wedding. Her pain must have been compounded when she learned that the groom's mother, Sarah Lee, had secretly accompanied the couple to the county seat of Junction and signed the certificate as witness to the union.[2]

In 1891 the number of people living in the 18-by-18-foot cabin was nine. Ethalinda had nearly died while giving birth to Myrtle, who would become the family historian. Ethalinda began to hemorrhage and was too weak to awaken her husband. A friend who was sheltering from the cold at the cabin heard her faint cries. He rousted George, and the two men did what they could to help the suffering woman. They prayed mightily that Ethalinda would survive.

The couple's thirteen-year-old son, William, raced his horse five miles in the snow to Teasdale and returned with a midwife. William liked to brag that it was the fastest and coldest ride of his life. Ethalinda

---

1. Both Leah and Walter's fathers had been imprisoned together at the Utah Territorial Penitentiary. Walter's father, John D. Lee, was awaiting trial for his role in the Mountain Meadows Massacre (of which we will hear more later) while Leah's biological father, William Phelps, was serving time for stealing horses. Lee recorded in his journal that he began holding classes at the prison after William asked for lessons on reading and writing.

2. Walter and Leah Lee were happily married for nearly fifty years. Walter built a spacious two-story home for Leah and their ten children on Main Street in Torrey. The Lee home is now a shop selling goods created by local artists, called The Old House. It is a short walking distance from the Morrill cabin.

remained in frail health after the birth.

In 1893, George built an addition to the cabin, doubling its size. Outside, he nailed narrow boards to the plank walls to cover gaps between the adjoining rooms. The Morrills' home had few comforts. It never had electricity, a bathroom, kitchen, icebox, washing machine, flush toilet, or a tub with running water. Myrtle remembered her mother laying out a hand-woven rag rug over layers of straw for warmth during the winter. The rug was put away in the summertime to help it last longer. The task of cleaning the wood floors fell to Myrtle, who took two or three days to scrub the floor with white sand from the creek because the family couldn't spare what little soap they had.

Unlike other settlements, no creek or stream ran through the bench. George Morrill, a water board member, was the first to receive a certificate for water shares, based on time digging ditches. Credits toward shares were pegged at $4 a day for eight hours of work for laborers bringing their own teams of horses. It would take nearly twenty years of digging before water flowed to all homesteads from the nearest spring, located ten miles away.

Maintaining canals required more work. Ditches had to be cleared of silt, banks repaired, and weeds burned to keep irrigation water flowing. There's an old saying that when farmers in the West are working on ditches, Easterners, enjoying more rainfall, have time to paint fences and barns.

In addition to his community duties, George Morrill frequently left home to work for his father and brothers in neighboring Piute County—a four-day round-trip ride. Their daughter Myrtle remembered that Ethalinda felt slighted when George never thought to ask what she needed when his family paid him in bartered goods.

Although Ethalinda's daughter Leah lived close by, Ethalinda endured long periods of isolation. Settlers who had joined them in Poverty Flat moved elsewhere when work stalled on a canal to the Fremont River, nicknamed the Dirty Devil. Ethalinda's parents, John and Margaret Young, who founded the town with the Morrills, gave up four years later and moved eighty miles north to Sevier County.

Before John Young left the settlement, he promised his water rights to outside ranchers, which would have doomed Poverty Flat. But George persuaded Young to transfer the rights to his stepson Charles Lee who, with some other investors, sold smaller, more affordable shares to townspeople, costing $5 each.

To ease her loneliness during George's frequent absences, Ethalinda spent her egg money on a 25-cent annual subscription to *Comfort* magazine. Family stories say George objected to Ethalinda spending what little cash they had on such an extravagance. But she ignored him and collected enough magazines to eventually insulate an entire room, ceiling, and outside cooking shed.

The magazine was progressive in the tightknit, patriarchal community. One column advised women to spend their egg money as they chose. "The cash received is her special perquisite," it said. "With the 'egg money' she buys her dresses and a few simple luxuries that signify so much to her in the way of comfort."

Some stories reported on women politicians and gave advice to girls seeking careers. Future nurses were advised to write to American Red Cross founder Clara Barton, whose address was simply Washington, D.C. Contests offered cash, starting at fifty cents. Prizes, books, and toys were offered for readers selling one or two subscriptions.[3]

---

3. *Comfort* highlighted articles on technology as well. In 1896 the magazine featured a hot-air contraption with components of a bicycle and a pneumatic baby carriage. "It has for sometime been prophesied that the bicycle will be superseded by the flying-machine. And already J.C. Rider (has) built a new machine which promises to revolutionize the 'science' of aerial navigation. Mr. Ryder has actually flown (ten miles) on his aerial bicycle from Hempstead to Richmond Hill (NY)."

September 1896 issue of Comfort *magazine.*

Comfort could be saucy for its time. One 1901 advice column scolded an unhappy reader in love with an uncaring man. "Why in the name of common sense do you love a man who tells you he doesn't care for you and treats you like a rag? Have some spirit about you and throw him over the fence."

One story tells of a love-sick schooner captain engaged for thirty years to a woman who refuses to marry while caring for her parents. There's also a pair of women detectives solving the mysterious kidnapping of two heirs. They all marry in a lavish ceremony at the Mansion House. And there's the story of a newspaper telegraph editor who remembers a romantic evening with his lost love over dinner, the scent of "boiled cabbage over violets" wafting across the room.

Ethalinda dressed plainly, although she pasted dozens of women's fashion pages to insulate her walls from the catalog John M. Smyth (a Chicago competitor to Sears, Roebuck & Co.). She frequently wore

August 1900 issue of Comfort *magazine.*

a long-sleeved white blouse, a dark-colored skirt that nearly touched the floor, and an apron tied at her waist. George's sister-in-law often sent old coats to Ethalinda, who couldn't afford one of her own. Ethalinda wove straw hats and knitted hoods, mittens, and stockings for needed cash or goods, often in the dark of night because she could not afford candles.

In 1897, the Morrills' daughter, Alice, was married during an intermission at a dance in neighboring Teasdale. The petite, blonde Alice was not quite sixteen and madly in love with a 19-year-old cowboy named David Teeples. He was six-foot-one with coal-black hair.[4]

Although the Morrills owned little more than their homestead, they donated a parcel for a church/school in 1898, allowing them and their neighbors to worship and educate their children near home. The old Torrey Log Church-School became the town's symbol. The landmark on Main Street, sitting kitty-corner to the Morrill cabin, is listed on the National Historic Register as a rare surviving example of log construction.[5]

The Morrills' eldest son, William,[6] married in 1901. Their young-

---

4. The marriage seems to have been a happy one. The Teeples's children remember hearing their parents giggling and talking well into the night. Alice, pregnant with her sixth child, died during the influenza pandemic in 1918, leaving behind five young children.

5. The old church/school was so small that during dances, tickets with numbers were handed out, allowing townspeople to share the wood-plank floor. Numbers were called out so that one group could dance—say a quadrille or a waltz—while the others waited their turn outside. Anne Snow, *Rainbow Views: A History of Wayne County*, 264.

6. Will Morrill's son Merlin was a forgiving man. Merlin was severely beaten and his wife Ellen murdered in 1971 at their Salt Lake County home during the Christmas holidays. A burglar beat to death his 60-year-old wife and ambushed Merlin when he returned from farm chores. The man was sentenced to life in prison but because of technicalities, was released after seven years in prison. Merlin said he would not

*Ethalinda Morrill with daughter Alice
and son William.*

est son, Alfred, wed in 1907. George Morrill officiated at the ceremony, but true to form, he simply recorded the date. Alfred, who was too shy to attend school after his older brother left for a job, moved 135 miles away to the desert town of Delta to find work.[7]

In his journals, George recorded scant details of any family member, but when he mentioned Ethalinda, he called her his "Dear Wife."

---

allow bitterness and hatred to harm his family. He comforted the killer's heartbroken parents and spoke of his faith that God would make his family whole.

7. During World War II, the U.S. government built an internment camp outside Delta to imprison more than 8,000 Japanese-Americans. The camp, named Topaz, was one of ten American incarceration centers.

George and Ethalindas' sons (from left) William Morrill and Alfred Morrill, and sons-in-law James Clarence Huntsman (Myrtle Morrill), and David Teeples (Alice Morrill).

Yet in 1914, the Morrills separated, George deeding the homestead to Ethalinda.

Myrtle suggested that one cause for her parents' estrangement was a "willful and headstrong" trait they all shared. "Because Ma and Pa were somewhat that way themselves and most of us inherited some of it, we were not without our difficult times," she wrote.

George lived with their children while doing chores on their farms. One granddaughter remembered George sleeping in a tent next to her family's two-room cabin.

Ethalinda and George came together in one last act of generosity. In 1915 the couple donated two acres of land for an elementary school, which operated from 1917 to 1954. Today, the majestic two-story stone school on Center Street is the Torrey Schoolhouse B&B Inn, which is directly north of the Morrill cabin. The old schoolyard is a city park.

Months before George's passing in 1919, Alice, on her deathbed during the flu pandemic, begged her parents to reunite. She placed her own wedding ring on Ethalinda's finger to ensure her parents would be together with her in the eternities. George kept his promise and came home to Ethalinda, but a lifetime of heavy labor caused his health to deteriorate. George Morrill died from edema on January 22, 1919. He was sixty-one.[8]

Ethalinda was alone. Her children had their own families, and some had moved away. She had suffered many heartbreaks during her lifetime. Her 18-year-old brother, Willis, died in a horse accident in 1878. Her 40-year-old brother, Alma Darius, drowned in 1905 while crossing the San Juan River. In 1912, her sister Lillian May died from a ruptured appendix, leaving a husband and seven young children. Ethalinda also outlived ten of her grandchildren.

In her later years, Ethalinda was able to buy a hand-cranked Kimball phonograph and a small collection of spindle records. Her favorites were "Listen to the Mocking Bird" and "Beautiful Isle of Somewhere." Its lyrics begin: "Somewhere the sun is shining, Somewhere the songbirds dwell; Hush, then, thy sad repining, God lives, and all is well."

Ethalinda's final portrait reveals a shy, perhaps melancholy smile. Her white hair is swept back in a proper bun, but a few tendrils are loose and still wavy. A granddaughter described Ethalinda as a small,

---

8. In the 1990s, descendants of Ethalinda's daughter by William Phelps, Leah, received permission from the Mormon Church for Ethalinda to posthumously be "sealed" (married) to her first husband in the hereafter. This makes Ethalinda a heavenly polyandrist since George had received that same promise more than a century earlier when he and Ethalinda were married in the St. George Temple. Although this is an unusual situation in Mormonism, the faithful believe relationships will be worked out in the hereafter.

The old Torrey Schoolhouse (now the Torrey Schoolhouse B&B Inn) sits on land donated by George and Ethalinda Morrill.
Credit: Maura Naughton.

slender woman, not quite five feet tall, with lots of dark auburn hair. She had big, pretty gray eyes, delicate hands, and skin that had a lovely sheen to it. In her last years, Ethalinda was still beautiful.

Her granddaughter Cleo Behunin described their final meeting. "The last time I saw her, she was standing in the orchard. She looked lonely as she waved goodbye to us."

Ethalinda died of pneumonia on October 18, 1933. She was seventy-nine.

In her obituary, the *Millard County Chronicle* noted her husband and father built the first houses on what was called "The Bench since changed to Torrey." Yet she had lived the longest in Torrey—fifteen years more than her husband and thirty-three years longer than her father.

All that remains of the Morrills' years in Poverty Flat is the sturdy cabin George built on harsh, rocky land, situated in one of the world's most scenic places. The cabin gave up one secret about Ethalinda. Buried beneath layers of plaster were scraps of *Comfort* pages that she pasted to the walls as insulation. My research showed what she saw: women in exquisite gowns attending elaborate balls, woman richly attired playing a leisurely game of tennis, and a bride dressed in expensive Brussels lace just before her wedding.

Ethalinda had never ventured beyond the Utah frontier. But she had always loved beauty. And romantic fantasies.

CHAPTER SIX
Land of the Sleeping Rainbow

"The whole country is a region of naked rock of many colors with cliffs and buttes about us and towering mountains in the distance."

—JOHN WESLEY POWELL
explorer, 1869

Visitors traveling to Capitol Reef can still see the same landscape that George Morrill first came upon in the early 1880s. As he guided his horse through a narrow gorge, the land suddenly opens into a geological wonder. Nearly a century later, the lands would be designated as one of Utah's Mighty Five National Parks. It features towering sandstone colonnades stacked together in undulating rows that disappeared into the horizon. The bright red formations are reminiscent of colossal temples built by the biblical pharaohs.

Locals call this unfolding panorama The Red Gate.

To the north stands the 11,300-foot Thousand Lake Mountain, and to the south looms Boulder Mountain, which sits atop the highest timbered plateau in North America. In the distance to the east are the rugged Henry Mountains, which in 1872 were the last range in the Lower 48 to be mapped.

At Capitol Reef, Navajo sandstone domes and craggy cliffs dominate the landscape. The high-stepped lands are bereft of forests, exposing the formations' deep underpinnings. The passage of time is etched onto broken outcroppings, down to strata deposited eons before the age of dinosaurs. Winter snows outline the giant peaks, making them appear to lunge forward. Hues of red, orange, yellow, purple, cream, and green color the layers of time.[1] People unaccustomed to the colossal formations often feel vulnerable and overwhelmed when they first encounter them.

Inside the park are wonders such as Temples of the Sun and Moon, Glass Mountain, Golden Throne, Chimney Rock, Factory Butte, and Capitol Dome, from which the park takes part of its name. Reef refers to its rocky cliffs which form a gigantic barrier to travel, similar to an ocean reef.

In 1854 explorer John C. Fremont marched through the area[2] while scouting for a northern transcontinental route for the railroad. For a long time, mystery surrounded whether his expedition had gone through Capitol Reef since virtually all the three hundred daguerreotypes taken during the journey were destroyed in an 1881 warehouse fire.

The mystery was solved 145 years later when a New Mexico photographer thought that perhaps an engraving made from one of the lost daguerreotypes depicted pinnacles at Capitol Reef. He wondered if the engraving had been made from a reversed image, which was why no one could pinpoint the peaks. When the image was set aright, park officials identified three oblasts, locally nicknamed Mom, Pop, and Henry. Fremont had indeed explored the park's Cathedral Valley.[3]

Oldtimers knew Fremont had traveled through the area decades

---

1. The geologic term for the area, waterpocket fold, seems a tepid description for the majestic 100-mile long upthrust that rises from the depths of the Earth's crust.

2. Today's Wayne County, Utah.

3. Lee Kruetzer, *Utah Preservation Magazine*, 20–21.

before. Fremont's men carved his name on a quaking aspen at Allred Point, about fifteen miles west of Torrey, to mark where the expedition had buried a cache of supplies to be retrieved later.[4] Although Native Americans raided the site, the tree stood for years. Individual aspens usually live fifty to sixty years, but in some parts of the West they can

Temple of the Sun in Cathedral Valley, Capitol Reef National Park. Credit: NPS/Chris Roundtree.

survive for as long as 150 years. Historian Steve Taylor recorded memories of elderly settlers, including his grandfather, who said they had seen the carving long before the tree died. The grove can still be seen in the distance from State Route 24, the Scenic Byway to Capitol Reef.

John Wesley Powell, known for boating down the Grand Canyon and giving the Colorado Plateau its name, also explored Utah. Topographer Almon Thompson led a Powell survey team through Capitol Reef during an 1871–72 expedition.

After the Powell expedition to Capitol Reef, isolated homesteads

4. The area is part of the Old Spanish Trail, a 700-mile trade route from New Mexico to Southern California. The trail also ran through Arizona, Colorado, Nevada, and Utah.

Chimney Rock, Capitol Reef National Park.
Credit: NPS/Chris Roundtree.

began appearing along a nearby 7,000-foot elevation named Rabbit Valley. The town of Thurber (later named Bicknell) was settled in 1875, and Fremont the next year (named for the famous explorer). In 1878, Teasdale and Loa[5] were founded. The latter town was named by an LDS missionary who had served in Hawaii. Loa means high, large, and powerful. East Loa (Lyman) was settled in 1879, Grover in 1880,

---

5. In 1892 the town of Loa became the county seat of the newly created Wayne County. The designation cut two days of riding to a neighboring county down to a few hours to file on a homestead, marry, purchase property, or conduct other legal business.

and finally Poverty Flat in 1886.

For years, Poverty Flat was on the brink of becoming another failed settlement, like the neighboring towns of Aldridge, Caineville, Notom, Blue Valley, Clifton, and Mesa. Even Fruita was abandoned despite perpendicular sandstone cliffs that sheltered the farmers' orchards.[6]

Poverty Flat seemed an apt name for the struggling settlement. Winds swept down from the mountains, which provided no shelter. Church leader Joseph Eckersley recorded this in his journal for December 1894: "I never experienced so severe a cold freezing wind in my life as I Encountered crossing Poverty Flat." In July 1895, he recorded an unexpected storm: "On reaching Poverty Flat we experienced a great change of climate, so cold we could not keep warm under a quilt."[7]

Poverty Flat received its official name of Torrey in 1898 when the town opened its first post office. The name honored Jay L. Torrey, a Wyoming state senator who called for volunteer cavalry regiments of cowboys and stockmen to fight in the Spanish-American War.[8] Many westerners answered the call and prepared to fight, but few were sent to Cuba.[9]

---

6. Fruita was absorbed into Capitol Reef National Park, where tourists now pick fruits, nuts, berries, and grapes on the pioneers' old homesteads.

7. Eckersley often stayed at the Morrill cabin during his many ecclesiastical visits. He recorded George and Ethalinda gifting him fruit they picked from their orchard. Eckersely's journal shows the bench was commonly known as Poverty Flat, although later histories claimed other names, such as Youngsville for Ethalinda Morrill's father, John Young, Central, Popular, and Bonita.

8. Today a great-grandnephew of the senator operates the Torrey Trading Post on Main Street.

9. The most famous volunteers, the Rough Riders, were commanded by future U.S President Teddy Roosevelt. The men took heavy losses when they stormed Cuba's San Juan Hill.

Slowly, Torrey began to prosper. The *Salt Lake Herald* reported that settlers had opened two blacksmith shops, and a small dry goods store, located in a private home. The December 1899 article noted that the town "had more bustle than almost any other small settlement for miles around, yet in July 1898, it was nothing more than a ranch."

Poverty Flat survived because of hard digging to get water to the struggling outpost. Beneath layers of plaster on the walls of the Morrill cabin, I uncovered portions of an 1899 soils map published by the newly created U.S. Department of Agriculture. The agency had sent chemists to valleys in Utah, New Mexico, Maryland, and Connecticut to analyze soils. George Morrill used the Utah map, though it depicted only Salt Lake Valley, to help determine where to dig canals and which soils would increase crop yields. When newer maps became available, the 1899 survey was used as insulation in the cabin walls. Today that map is framed and mounted where I found it on the bedroom's north wall.[10]

In 1910, Torrey opened its first stand-alone store on Main Street, directly south of the Morrill cabin. The store was named Wayne Umpire,[11] perhaps because of the spirited talk that went on around it. Outside, men lounged on a bench or sat on stumps of petrified logs. They carved small pieces of wood and sometimes argued. Spats seemed common. In a 1909 journal entry, church leader Eckersley told of a two-hour meeting in Torrey to resolve differences "after much counsel and exhortation."

---

10. I called different agencies in the USDA to track down the history of the surveys. But agencies changed names and departments, making it difficult to track. After weeks of research, I located a man, David L. Lindbo, who is co-author of *Know Soil, Know Life*. The book on soil surveys quotes Henry David Thoreau on the complexities of ordinary dirt: "Heaven is under our feet as well as over our heads."

11. The store was renamed the Chuckwagon. It is now located on Main Street in the center of Old Town.

The store accepted payment in eggs, considered nearly as good as cash. For years, Ethalinda Morrill sold eggs for cash or bartered goods.[12] Bulk foods, dry goods, bullets, and dynamite were displayed behind the front counter. Clerks sent money in an overhead, hand-operated tram up to the second floor where the cash was stored. Change and a receipt were tucked into a canister, which was propelled back downstairs by gravity.

The store's owner was E. P. "Port" Pectol, who ran the business with his beloved Dot and their four daughters.[13] The Pectols lived at the store to begin with but eventually built a home next door. As a Mormon bishop (pastor), Pectol opened the store and his home for funerals and viewings.

Pectol envisioned economic opportunities in the colorful desert and mountains surrounding Torrey. In 1921 he formed a booster club to push for state and later federal protections of what would become Capitol Reef National Monument. He and his legislator brother-in-law Joseph Hickman called it Wayne's Wonderland. Tragically, Joseph Hickman drowned in 1925—days after they celebrated a gathering of politicians who might help set aside the lands for the public to enjoy. A majestic arch called Hickman Bridge is named after him.

Pectol also amassed a collection of ancient Fremont Indian artifacts he had unearthed in the Capitol Reef region. He displayed the relics upstairs at the store where visitors could view the collection for free. He often told of the time in 1926 when he came upon his most extraordinary find.

Earlier, a rancher named Earl Behunin was looking for lost sheep when he stopped under an overhanging cliff during a rainstorm. He

---

12. George and Ethalinda Morrill lived next door to the store and shopped there. I discovered wrapping papers stamped with the store's name in the walls of the cabin that were used as insulation.

13. Later an infant son would be adopted into the family.

spotted some leather strings protruding from the ground. When he dug around them, he found a robe with moccasins and an unusual hat tucked inside. The hat and the markings on the robe reminded him of special clothing Mormons wear in their temple ceremonies. Since the Book of Mormon tells of a tribe of Lamanites, who were presented as ancestors of today's Native Americans, the relics seemed to prove the authenticity of the Book of Mormon.

Behunin reported his finding to Pectol who was his bishop. He then took Pectol to the site, located in the Sand Creek drainage area in today's Capitol Reef. There, Pectol saw something that appeared to be rawhide. When he lifted the object, he saw that it was an ancient buffalo-hide shield. Pectol dug deeper and was astounded to discover two more uniquely painted leather shields. He went home and returned with his family to the site. "For the space of what seemed to me two or three minutes, no one seemed to breathe; we were so astonished," Pectol wrote. "We felt we were in the presence of the one who had buried the shields."

According to family lore, the famed novelist Zane Grey saw Pectol's collection while traveling through Torrey.[14] Grey estimated the shields alone were worth $30,000 at the time. Now, they are considered priceless.

Early settlers and ranchers augmented their incomes by digging up Native American artifacts and selling them. Congress passed the 1906 Antiquities Act to protect Native American artifacts and ruins, which whites had been looting. President Teddy Roosevelt signed the act, and

---

14. Grey remembered visiting Capitol Reef with 14 friends during a 1929 stop at Richfield. The *Richfield Reaper* gave as much space to an interview with the famous novelist as it did to naming the garage that serviced the cars and the harness shop where Grey purchased riding gloves. Grey said of the Capitol Reef country: "The finest one-day ride I ever had was from the Capitol Gorge to Hanksville," about 50 miles east of Torrey.

in 1908 set aside the Grand Canyon as a reserve to stop pillaging, mining, and development.[15]

Pectol's family donated the bulk of his collection—including the robe Behunin had discovered—to the Utah State University Eastern

Credit: Steve Jorgensen

Prehistoric Museum in Price. The collection includes a rare unfired clay figurine in a miniature cradleboard, baskets, pottery, and a spoon made from the horn of a bighorn sheep. Among several tools is a deer antler with a hole in it, used to straighten the shaft of an arrow. A portion of the Fremont collection was donated by descendants of Charles Lee, a son of the infamous John D. Lee.[16]

15. Pot hunters still dig up treasures on public lands for profit. Illegal digs destroy critical information about the relic, destroy its provenance, and show a profound disrespect to Native Peoples.

16. Western writer Wallace Stegner described Charles as an old-time, zealous Mormon who found buried artifacts through heavenly dreams. After Charles' death in

Utah Governor and War Secretary George Dern.
Used by permission, Utah State Historical Society.

Decades later, the National Park Service turned over the shields to the Navajo Nation, headquartered in Window Rock, Arizona. The Fremont people, who created the shields, lived in Utah and parts of Nevada, Idaho, and Colorado from about 1,500 to 700 years ago. They built small villages and pit houses, planted corn and squash, harvested wild plants, and hunted. It's believed that a prolonged drought may have driven them from their homes.

1941, much of the collection was dispersed and essentially disappeared. Wallace Stegner, *Mormon Country*, page 157–158.

In 1933, Port was elected to the state legislature. He immediately asked President Franklin D. Roosevelt to create "Wayne's Wonderland." Utah had a powerful friend in convincing Roosevelt to declare it a national monument—War Secretary George Dern, a former Utah governor, grandfather of actor Bruce Dern, and great-grandfather of actor Laura Dern. George's friendship with Roosevelt was so close that the President's wife, Eleanor, was Bruce Dern's godmother.

In 1937 Roosevelt signed a proclamation designating nearly 38,000 acres as Capitol Reef National Monument. The monument was placed under the control of Zion National Park.[17]

In 1971 President Nixon set aside Capitol Reef as a National Park.

"At Capitol Reef nature has taken ordinary raw materials (rocks), painted in a spectrum of rainbow hues, and shaped them into a work of amazing erosional intricacy," wrote author Ward J. Roylance. "Maze, tangle and labyrinth are descriptive terms that are eminently suitable here. So are adjectives such as strange, marvelous, exquisite, harmonious, majestic—the list could go on without exaggeration."[18]

Today Roylance's Torrey home—just down the street from the old Morrill cabin—is headquarters to the nonprofit Entrada Institute, located on the newly named Historic Poverty Flat Road. For more than thirty years, two generations of the Scholl family have improved the property. The family has supported the Institute, which is dedicated to the arts and preserving the historical and cultural heritage of the Colorado Plateau. This high desert is home to the Utah's Mighty Five National Parks (Capitol Reef, Zion, Bryce Canyon, Canyonlands, and Arches), Colorado's

---

17. I found a reminder of the designation at the Morrill cabin when I came across the top of a wooden crate, addressed to Capitol Reef with the return address listed as Zion.

18. Ward J. Roylance, "An Introduction to the Park," *The Capitol Reef Reader*, edited by Stephen Trimble (Salt Lake City: University of Utah Press, 2019), 110.

Mesa Verde, and Arizona's Petrified Forest and Grand Canyon.

George and Ethalinda Morrill could not have imagined the town they founded would become a gateway to millions of visitors to one of America's great national parks. But the colorful geologic wonders that drew the Morrills to Poverty Flat attracted many other admirers who have worked to protect a place Navajos called Land of the Sleeping Rainbow.

Margaret Young

CHAPTER SEVEN
A Woman of Faith, A Woman of Grief

"They had at least a partial separation and (Margaret Young) still hoped to have her first love in the eternities instead of Grandfather. She felt that after the hardships she had endured, she was entitled to a little consideration."
—MARY ANN YOUNG SMITH
Margaret Young's granddaughter

Ethalinda's mother, Margaret Young, helped open Poverty Flat and many other frontier settlements. She frequently lived in makeshift, temporary shelters while bearing several children—all without complaint. She also endured a long, seemingly loveless marriage.

Margaret had lived a life dictated by the choices men made for her. The first of these fateful choices was her father's decision to arrange her marriage, even though Margaret was in love with a man she had met while crossing the American plains to the Utah Territory.

Ethalinda and her mother Margaret were close, and each seemed to spend their lives pining the loss of an early, lost love, according to the recollections of their respective granddaughters.

Margaret's father, William Young, and his brother Alfred Young had an unbreakable bond. They served an LDS Church mission to a region of Tennessee known for its hostility toward Mormons and then fled with the Saints after mobs attacked the Mormon city of Nauvoo, Illinois. The brothers lived in the same hamlet in Utah Territory, and each named a son after the other. They believed that they alone should decide whom their respective son and daughter should marry and felt certain that their children should marry each other.

So, on May 19, 1850, Ethalinda Margaret Young was married to her first cousin, John William Young, in her parents' home in the Cottonwood neighborhood of Salt Lake Valley. John D. Lee, a longtime friend of the family, officiated.[1] In what seemed a romantic twist to her father, Margaret did not have to change her surname.[2]

Margaret's firstborn, William Alfred, named for her father and uncle, died just short of his first birthday. Ethalinda was born in 1854. Three year later, while they were living in Provo, about forty miles south of Salt Lake City, John joined Mormon militiamen. The men intended to stop U.S. Army troops from marching into Salt Lake City in what became known as the Mormon War. Family lore says Ethalinda's father had not been assigned to the dangerous military duty. He volunteered. He left Margaret behind with a nine-month-old baby and Ethalinda, then a three-year-old toddler. Thousands of Mormon men left for the same reason, leaving the arduous task of spring planting and fall harvesting to the women and children.[3]

John and upwards of 2,000 Mormons made the high-walled Echo Canyon, which led into Salt Lake City, inaccessible to the army by building a system of breastworks, rifle pits, and dams. They also piled up rocks to roll down onto the invading soldiers. These, along with

---

1. Seven years later, he would participate in the infamous Mountain Meadows Massacre.

2. Their marriage was later solemnized in Salt Lake City during a sacred ceremony that promised their union would endure into the eternities.

3. Much of Utah Territory was made up of high desert with rocky soils, arid lands, and a short growing season.

the Mormons' daring raids and deep winter snows, forced the Army to winter at Fort Bridger, a fur-trading post in present-day Wyoming. But the Mormons burned the fort, forcing the U.S. soldiers to suffer through the winter. However, the soldiers' commander, Col. Albert Sidney Johnston, was able to keep his supply lines open and, through a series of negotiations, assure Mormon leaders that they would be granted full pardons if they submitted to federal authority.[4]

Mormon prophet Brigham Young had no choice but to accept a pardon. The Army estimated the Mormon leader could field a militia of 7,000 men, with only 1,000 of them being expert horsemen and marksmen.[5] The remainder of the militiamen were farmers and craftsmen, untrained to fight in a war. By contrast, Johnston commanded cavalry, infantry, and artillery units, and had approval for a force of 5,000 soldiers—one-third the size of the entire U.S. Army. Even with fortifications in Echo Canyon, the Army could have easily overcome the Mormons with only five hundred men.[6]

With peace established, John Young returned to Provo. Then, in 1858, with Margaret pregnant with their fourth child, Brigham Young (no relation to Margaret and John), in desperate need of carpenters and blacksmiths, called John to help open outlying settlements. First, they moved 260 miles south to Santa Clara, near the Utah-Nevada border. There, John built a makeshift shelter for his family, which would be

---

4. Johnston joined the Confederacy during the Civil War and was mortally wounded at the Battle of Shiloh in 1862.

5. Some of these men had served in the Mormon Battalion, a volunteer unit that reinforced U.S. troops during the Mexican-American War from 1846–1848. Their military scout was Jean-Baptiste Charbonneau—son of the famed Sacagawea. The Shoshone mother was pregnant with her son during the 1804–1806 Lewis and Clark Expedition, an 8,000-mile trek from the Louisiana Territory to the Pacific Northwest.

6. David L. Bigler and Will Bagley, *The Mormon Rebellion: America's First Civil War 1857–1858* (Norman: University of Oklahoma Press, 2011), 320–322.

among the thirty-five shelters and temporary houses Margaret lived in during her lifetime. She never enjoyed a permanent home.

Soon, John was serving as a missionary to nearby American Indian tribes under the leadership of Jacob Hamblin. In 1860 John took Hamblin's fifteen-year-old daughter, Maryette, as a plural wife. She was seventeen years his junior. Margaret's only choice was to support her

Brigham Young
Used by permission: Utah State Historical Society

husband's polygamous marriage. If she rebelled, she was taught that she risked eternal damnation. Ethalinda was six years old at the time and likely understood some of the difficulties this new marriage inflicted on her mother.

A few months after marrying Maryette, John moved Margaret fifty miles north to the village of Pinto. There, John pitched a tent for Margaret and piled posts and willows next to it, which acted as a lean-to where she could cook. The time he spent with Maryette in Santa Clara, and his travels to convert Hopis and Navajo on the Utah-Arizona border, took him away from Margaret for long periods of time.

One night while John was away, Margaret heard footsteps outside her tent. She stacked stools near the canvas entrance and placed pans atop each piece of furniture, hoping the noise would awaken her if someone came in. Still hearing footsteps, she fired three shots through the tent top, scaring away the intruders and terrifying Ethalinda and her other children.

In Pinto, Margaret would give birth to four babies. Maryette gave birth to three daughters before she separated from John.[7]

Margaret endured her greatest hardships in the late 1860s when Brigham Young called them to help settle the Big Muddy Mission. The settlement was situated in the Mojave Desert, northeast of Las Vegas. It was a hot, barren land dotted with tall thorny succulents called Joshua trees, and stunted mesquite or devil bushes. The settlement was charged with growing cotton as part of the LDS Church's plan to gain self-sufficiency. But settlers lacked the manpower to dig adequate irrigation ditches and had constant trouble with Paiutes who stole livestock, partly in retaliation for the Mormons taking over their choice lands near the river.

"There was no gold field in their mind's eye, not even a land of milk and honey," Wallace Stegner wrote of the Big Muddy Mission. "They were headed for a desert outpost where the chances were fifty-fifty they

---

7. Shortly after Maryette's separation from John Young, she became the third plural wife of William Bailey Maxwell, a man twenty-four years her senior. Maxwell served as a captain in the Mormon militia fighting U.S. Army troops during the 1857 Utah War. Maryette bore him ten children, bringing the number of Maxwell's offspring to twenty-five.

would starve to death. Still they went, and they went singing."[8]

The Youngs' son Alpheus told a granddaughter that the first house he could recall was a willow shanty located on the Muddy River. He remembered the early settlers had little bread but plenty of milk, butter, and cheese from their dairy cows. John Young tanned cowhides with red pine bark to make shoes for his children. Cat hide was tanned and used for shoestrings.

Flash floods, sands that could not hold dams, isolated markets, and an inability for the settlers to adapt to the extreme environment doomed the settlement. When Brigham Young visited the mission in 1870, he gave the settlers permission to abandon it. Many already had. That fall, a flood wiped out John and Margaret Young's home.[9]

"It is remarkable that the settlers of the Muddy Mission maintained their communities as long as they did," wrote scholar Monique Elaine Kimball. "For five years they battled the arid land, manipulated a limited water supply and futilely chased Paiutes who stole livestock. They were challenged by fever, fire, drought, and flood which devastated their small resources. Their cotton produced relatively little profit. Some settlers could have been considered materially wealthy when they arrived, but few improved their circumstances by the time they left."[10]

After the collapse of the Big Muddy Mission,[11] the Youngs traveled 150 miles northeast to the newly settled Kanab in Kane County, Utah, where Margaret gave birth to her tenth child. The land was arid

8. *Mormon County*, 112.

9. According to the 1870 Census, the Young family lived in a now-defunct county called Rio Virgin in the Utah Territory.

10. Monique Elaine Kimball, "A Matter of Faith: A Study of the Muddy Mission" (master's thesis: University of Nevada Las Vegas, 1988), 49.

11. In 1855, Brigham Young also sent Mormons to establish a mission in Las Vegas Valley. The Old Mormon Fort was the first structure built by settlers in what would become Las Vegas.

but spectacular, being located within the Grand Circle, which includes Vermilion Cliffs National Monument, Bryce Canyon National Park, the North Rim of the Grand Canyon, Zion National Park, and Lake Powell. But within three years they moved on to Kanosh[12] in Millard County, where Margaret gave birth to their youngest two children, bringing the number of their surviving offspring to ten.

Still seeking more fertile farmlands and better sources of water, the Youngs moved eighty miles south to Circleville and then to neighboring Junction. In 1878, their youngest child, Willis James, 18, died after falling from a horse. They then moved to Loa,[13] where John built a gristmill, and then to Poverty Flat.

After John D. Lee's execution for his role in an attack on a wagon train, called the Mountain Meadows Massacre, John Young took one of his widows, Sarah Caroline Lee, as his plural wife. Sarah moved to the struggling Poverty Flat with a daughter and two sons. Family lore says Margaret was again unhappy with her husband's polygamous marriage, often having little food for her own children and enduring many of her husband's long absences.

The Youngs stayed in Poverty Flat for less than four years, soon moving eighty miles east to the tiny hamlet of Joseph. The Youngs' son Alma Darius and his bride, Amanda, followed. But, in 1890, Amanda died at twenty-four years old on Christmas Day, prompting Margaret to move into Alma's home to care for his four motherless children.

The following year, John died on December 31 at sixty-three years old. So, Margaret followed Alma's family to New Mexico, where he had opened a freight business. But that sojourn came to an end when Alma, his three boys, and three employees, who had loaded a freight wagon onto a ferry to cross the San Juan River were caught in a flood caused

---

12. Kanosh is located thirteen miles from Fillmore, the Territory's capital from 1851 to 1856.

13. George and Ethalinda Morrill followed them.

by a cloudburst upstream. The ferry's cables broke, setting it adrift in the raging waters. Alma helped his sons grab onto some willows near the shore where they jumped onto the bank, but he and his employees stayed on the ferry to save their cargo. The bodies of the four men were found weeks later, washed up on a sandbank.

Margaret took her four grandchildren to Monticello, Utah, to be near her son Alfred who owned and operated a gristmill and sawmill. In 1913 Alfred opened the region's first silent theater, affixed with lights from a generator he built. Before each showing, a boy walked around town shouting, "Show tonight! Young Theater!"

Grandmother Margaret raised her deceased son's four children to adulthood in Monticello. Virginia married and moved to Canada. Les punched cattle, busted broncos, and was known as one of the best horsemen in San Juan County. Jacob worked for an oil company and is buried in Monticello, where he lived most of his life. John Alma Young, named for his grandfather and father, lost his young wife and moved to California where he married a woman connected to my own family.

Elderly and frail, Margaret moved in with her children. A granddaughter wrote that Margaret stayed busy in her old age, spinning wool into yarn, and knitting sweaters, stockings, and other articles of clothing for her family. She had a tiny room with a small window which froze and became encrusted on the outside with snow, leaving her in the dark. To save fuel in her kerosene lamp, she used the warmth of her fingers to rub a small space on the windowpane that could let light in. She often knit in the dark to save candles, without dropping a stitch.

A daughter took Margaret to live with her family in Monticello, where she stayed in the front room. Margaret shared treats and loved to step dance into her 80s. Margaret refused help, did her own cooking, and usually arose first to wash her own clothes. One morning in May she was too tired to get up. On May 25, 1917, she quietly drifted off. She was eighty-five years old. Her granddaughters speculate that Margaret hoped to be united with her first love, rather than John, in the eternities.

It was Margaret who provided a familial link to my own ancestors, who lived a world away from the Utah frontier.

Grenz Family.
Girl in upper right is the author's maternal
grandmother, Elisabeth Grenz Huether.

CHAPTER EIGHT
Tears of My Ancestors

"Dear Brother, I wish we had some of the bread that we used to give to the horses at home. Now we eat anything."
> —A 1929 letter from a sister living in Ukraine to my grandfather, a farmer in North Dakota.

I was astonished one day to find out that I am distantly related (by marriage) to Ethalinda, through her mother, Margaret Young. Margaret's son, John Alma Young, married a widow named Edna Otto after he moved from Utah to California. Edna's maiden name is Grenz—the German surname of my grandmother Elisabeth. The two women grew up in North Dakota, about one hundred miles apart. Both had been among ethnic Germans who fled Russian persecution, settling in Canada and the American Midwest.

The persecutions went back to the 19th-century tsars and continued with the Soviets Joseph Stalin and Vladimir Lenin. These leaders ordered ethnic-cleansing pogroms or set up phony famines, exporting their victims' grain and livestock to distant parts of the empire, leaving them to starve. Some of these starving people's relatives tried to drive cattle across the border to feed their trapped families, but Stalin refused them entrance. Russia-Germans and Jews were executed, starved to death, or ordered to forced labor camps in the Gulag. When Stalin closed Russia's borders, many victims tried to flee through dangerous underground networks. In all, more than one million Russia-Germans were killed between 1915 and 1949.

Elisabeth, my grandmother, was one who had escaped. But life was harsh in the Midwest. Elisabeth had divorced her first husband, an alcoholic who regularly beat her. She ran away after he tried to stab her to death before he fell to the floor in a drunken stupor. Struggling to support three children (my mother's older half-sisters) in the frigid farm prairie lands of North Dakota, she needed a husband. Heinrich Huether, a widower with three children, was desperate for a wife.

They wed, but the marriage was not a happy one. Grandmother was illiterate, having grown up in the early twentieth century when education was a luxury the poorest immigrants could not afford. Accustomed to the company of educated women and resenting her illiteracy, Heinrich was cruel to her.

Mother remembered the day a letter arrived at her childhood home in Beulah, North Dakota, in the winter of 1929. It was mailed from a Ukrainian city near Odessa, once known as the Jewel of the Black Sea. Heinrich's widowed sister begged for money to save her family from starvation. Mother clearly remembered the pain on Heinrich's face as he silently read the letter.

In her letter, she described people starving to death in storms that sent temperatures plunging to twenty-six degrees below zero. Desperate villagers had broken into her attic, stealing what little food her family of five had possessed: seven pounds of white flour and three pounds of cornmeal.

A wealthy brother sent nothing, but Heinrich sent one dollar even though he was poor and would soon lose his own farm. His sister believed the money he sent was a miracle from God. Russian postal officers routinely tore open envelopes to steal the money inside. But Heinrich's letter with the one dollar somehow got through untouched. Heinrich lost contact with his sister after that. We only know that her son-in-law starved to death and a baby died. Many more violent pogroms against Russia-Germans and Jews would come.[1]

After Heinrich lost their farm and died during the Great Depression, Grandmother and their two youngest children (my mother and aunt) again faced hunger. My mother, Wanda Huether House, remembered hiding from classmates because her lunch sandwiches were wrapped in clean rags rather than wax paper. Some friends got dolls at Christmas while she was lucky to find an orange in her stocking. I once ran across a 1935 flier advertising her family's possessions for sale when the bank took over their farm: seven head of cattle, four horses, a wagon, a header to harvest grain, cultivator, plow, feed grinder, nine-foot drill, and several small tools. Her father never owned a tractor.

Mother had spoken Low German in her childhood home rather than the scholarly High German. This gave her mother-in-law ammunition to disrespect her. Neither woman knew that the dialect is named for the geographical region of Mother's ancestors. Mother was so ashamed of her language that sadly, she never taught us a single German word.

---

1. In 2016, a memorial was held in remembrance of a long-forgotten slaughter known as the Odessa Massacre of 1941. As many as 30,000 Jews were shot, tortured, or burned alive when Romanian and German troops controlled the city of my ancestors. The Russia-German neighbors in Ukraine also died in pogroms unleashed in 1932–33. The Ukrainian famine, known as the Holodomor for "starvation" and "to inflict death" left 3.9 million people dead.

In 2015 the Holodomor Memorial in Washington, D.C. opened to honor victims of the famine. The memorial was built by the National Park Service and the Ukrainian government. Because of the genocide against my own people, I felt a kinship with the Ukrainians who perished in the famine and with the brave people who are fighting Russian aggression today.

My mother carried psychological scars from her impoverished childhood; she seemed more comfortable with her austere childhood on the plains of North Dakota than her life in the prosperous Los Angeles area during the post-World War II boom. She was a survivor of the Great Depression and adhered to traits from this era. She believed in kinship, frugality, and making do with what one had—the same characteristics as the Morrill pioneers. Mother was best known among her grandchildren for her lectures on using too much toilet paper. She was also strict about wasting food. If I didn't eat my oatmeal covered with evaporated milk, she slid the bowl over a pilot light on the back of the oven to keep it warm. There would be no other food for the day until I ate my soggy, leftover breakfast. She once told my daughter Sarah that her biggest regret was never taking me in her arms.

When Grandmother moved in with us at our California home, neighbor boys called her a witch, which always led to fisticuffs with my brothers. Heavy labor had ravaged her petite body. She had broken or severely strained her back in a farm accident, and years of poor nutrition had weakened her bones. She had a dowager's hump so large that she was nearly bent over when she walked. Her world shrank to a living room couch and a room barely large enough for a small bed and nightstand.

I don't remember a time when we didn't adore her. After finding Dad's cigarette stash in the back of a closet, my brother Tom sneaked underneath Dad's bed to smoke one, lighting the mattress on fire. When Dad demanded to know the culprit, he was dumbfounded when our timid, devout grandmother insisted on taking the blame. After that, Tom began talking to Grandma after school. He might have grieved the deepest when he lost his boyhood confidant. I would name my first daughter Elisabeth in her honor and ultimately give her my grandmother's old Bible.

The lifelong poverty and hardships that afflicted my mother and grandmother reminded me of the lives of Margaret Young and her daughter, Ethalinda Morrill. But I found the lives of my sister and myself echoing theirs as well.

Lynette was my older sister. And like Ethalinda, was a voracious reader and a protector. She shielded my brothers and me from the perils that lurked within our own home, protected us from neighborhood bullies, and did not tolerate sibling fights. She did, however, beat us up when we dared call her Yippy. She suffered from eczema, and to keep her from scratching, Mom had tied her down in her crib. Her howls would eventually subside into whimpers that Mother said sounded like a dog yipping. Lynnette suffered throughout her childhood from outbreaks of eczema. Creams and lotions of the time exacerbated her condition. Her only relief was when I gently massaged her scarred joints, often at night as we fell asleep. In return, I bargained to borrow her clothes, thinking I could be as beautiful as she was.

I had always looked up to her. She began tending me as an infant when she was three years old.[2] She was eleven when she started cooking dinners for our family. Lynnette was fourteen years old when, after another bitter fight with Dad, Mother contacted Lynnette's biological father and told him to come meet his daughter for the first time. I was childishly angry that Lynnette had a family which didn't include me. She spent time comforting me without sharing her own pain. It would be years before I realized that she had learned about her biological father the same afternoon I had.

Only five years later, Lynnette's life would echo Ethalinda's again when her husband suddenly died after contracting an infection that destroyed his kidneys when organ transplants were rare. Ethalinda was twenty-one years old when she became a widow. Lynnette was only nineteen. Despite her grief over the death of her first husband, Lynnette comforted his grieving parents, remarried, and continued to care

---

2. Ethalinda's earliest memories were taking care of her siblings, starting when she was two years old.

for us. The first Christmas after Dad died, she decorated our home, bought presents, and cooked a holiday dinner before returning to her own young children.

Lynnette would guide me when my own marriage dissolved. My first husband left me only days after my brother Fred was killed in the line of duty. Though I was angry at his timing, she finally convinced me that he had done me a favor. Having left the LDS Church over issues of patriarchy, she showed me how my husband's insistence that he was the head of the home and prime decision-maker had affected our family. She also pointed out the burden of bread-winning he had shifted to me as he dropped one college major after another over our twenty-year marriage. As George had left Ethalinda physically to fend for herself, my husband's neglect of our relationship left me with the heavy responsibility of raising a family and maintaining a household. After he left me, my husband convinced our three youngest children I was crazy. I began drinking, proving his claim. Lynnette wouldn't tolerate these lapses in my judgment, no matter how much pain I felt. Although she lived hundreds of miles away, Lynnette could sense my worst days and would phone me. She sent humorous but poignant postcards nearly every day. For a year.

Lynnette encouraged me in my struggle to get work. I was the first in my family to graduate from college, though a brother-in-law had told me it was a shame that I was taking the place of a man who had to support a family. But Lynnette laughed off the remark, allowing me to see the humor in his silly, twisted thinking.

After college, I was repeatedly turned down for jobs at *The Salt Lake Tribune* despite my degree and several years of experience writing for four other publications. When a female editor finally hired me, her male supervisor asked about the wisdom of me leaving my five children to work. She replied, "Obviously, she's taken care of it, or she wouldn't have applied." The male supervisor's chauvinistic attitude was nothing new to me. I had spent twenty years in a marriage and culture where women were subservient to their husbands.

But the job was difficult. After my brother's death and divorce, I couldn't concentrate, sitting at my desk and silently weeping. One day a colleague named Paul Rolly happened by and asked what I was writing. After I summarized the story, he offered to write the lede—the first paragraph that describes the article's key points. Paul's help became a ritual. On the days I couldn't focus on a story, he dropped by to chat, and sometimes we went to lunch. For years, I reported to Lynnette on our growing friendship. I was nervous because of my previous failed relationship, but it helped that she respected Paul. I began to understand that I could trust him. I wanted to be with Paul, but I was terrified of marriage. Lynnette reassured me and explained that it could be difficult for unhappily married people to take another spouse.

It would be seven years before Paul and I married. When I handed out invitations to the inboxes of our *Tribune* colleagues, I was so worried that I forgot to include our names. "What the hell is this—and who the hell is getting married?" one reporter shouted in the newsroom. Colleagues worked up a mock newspaper page under the headline: "Paul Rolly's Jolly, He Got Himself New House." I had a temper, but Paul rarely lost his, so the story compared our unlikely relationship to "a meteorological event powerful enough to rip your shorts."

I was so apprehensive about our marriage ceremony that I nearly fainted. I could feel Lynnette's hand on my shoulder as she quietly talked to me: "We will now begin our deep breathing exercise." Paul patiently waited at the altar while Lynnette calmed me in the hallway.

Paul and I had nine children between us, which sometimes caused rifts. Most of them were teenagers who adjusted in different ways to the complexities of second marriages and combined families. It was Lynnette who taught me how to treat a husband. Once I called her from a friend's home after storming out on Paul. She told me to go home and talk, and

Paul listened. When we quarreled, Paul said Lynnette was his best ally.

Lynnette and I had a younger sister, fifteen years younger than Lynnette. When Mother became exhausted, Lynnette reared our sister alongside her own five children. Years later, I got a call from Lynnette, who was crying so hysterically I didn't know who was on the phone. Our sister had told Lynnette she wasn't invited to her wedding. She wanted to make a good impression on her fiancé and fretted that her cousins—including Lynnette's own children—would be too rowdy and not correctly attired. It reminded me of Ethalinda finding out that her eldest daughter had eloped.

The rift my younger sister's marriage caused in our family went deeper and deeper as time went on. She lived in an exclusive gated community and was eager to impress her wealthy neighbors. When her husband became gravely ill, Mother offered to come help take care of him. She insisted Mother place a sticker on her car window stamped "housekeeper." She also talked Mother into giving up her gravesite, which lies near our father's resting place. Mother supposedly agreed to be cremated nearly forty-five years after purchasing her burial plot.[3]

But it was Lynnette who died first, in 2009. She taught me how to die with dignity. When she was ill with pancreatic cancer, she insisted that doctors talk to her directly rather than her husband or me. "I'm also in the room," she said in a weak but firm voice when we unconsciously excluded her.

Lynnette gave her husband permission to remarry and instructed her children to support his decision. I gave Lynnette the only gift I could, letting her know I would be fine when she passed. In our last meeting, I said, "If there's an afterlife, I want you to be the one who comes for me."

She whispered, "Done."

---

3. Mother died in 2013. I used a small inheritance from her to buy the old Morrill cabin in Torrey.

CHAPTER NINE
Mothers, First and Always

A "mother, grandmother, an educator, and a business woman as well."
—Description of Utah's first female governor
and longtime politician Olene Walker,
The Salt Lake Tribune's 2003 Person of the Year award.

While I researched the history of the Morrill cabin, I learned that little has changed about the perception of women in Utah from the days when Ethalinda Morrill founded Poverty Flat. When the *Salt Lake Herald* ran a story in 1899, the reporter said George was the town founder —without mentioning Ethalinda. Tellingly, he had interviewed only Ethalinda because George was away at the time.

During the past century, we have witnessed giant leaps in technology and health care—but gender discrimination persists.

Ethalinda Morrill likely read about inequities facing women in several articles that appeared in *Comfort*, which she subscribed to and pasted to her cabin walls as insulation. "The secret of the surest short cut to success lies in the fingers and not in the face. (Yet) employers (are rare) who are willing to pay a man's wages to a woman even if she does more and better work," according to an 1892 article.

When I began to work as a journalist, my byline regularly appeared, making my career high-profile at a time when women were expected to remain in the home. Women who did work quietly took jobs to supplement family incomes. Some of my neighbors in conservative Utah County took jabs at women who worked.

Church meetings became painful when Sunday school teachers continually attacked women who, they said, worked to pay for extravagant vacations, expensive boats, and pricy recreational vehicles. Frankly, all the women I knew worked to feed their families. I decided that groceries, school clothes, and music lessons for my children were not unnecessary expenses.

I tired of feeling despondent after attending meetings of The Church of Jesus Christ of Latter-day Saints. When I dropped in on a meeting at a Presbyterian congregation, I heard messages of hope, compassion, and most of all, acceptance. My children continued to attend LDS meetings, and their lives were filled with a sense of community and purpose.

Ethalinda's escape from the stifling patriarchy was to marry an outlaw and taste the wild side of that era. My escape was to become a professional journalist and go to work for *The Salt Lake Tribune.* It was the state's largest newspaper, which was founded by rebels to create an alternate voice to the LDS Church-owned *Deseret News.*

I feared for the future of my daughters in this male-dominated society when I attended a workshop for high school girls in Salt Lake City. The speaker asked how many in the audience expected to work after they married. Few raised their hands, but nearly everyone acknowledged their own mothers worked outside the home.

My heart broke for those innocent girls. I knew they were unprepared for the likelihood they would have to work themselves. I had covered the same story over and over about girls opting out of advanced training but finding themselves in need of a good job—no matter their marital status.

I knew this from my own life. I was the breadwinner in my first marriage, and I had an education. I landed a job in journalism that I loved, but I earned less than my male counterparts, even after the *Tribune* nominated me for a Pulitzer Prize after I located historical documents in the Mark Hofmann forgery/murder investigation. I was paid so little that I had to juggle work as a correspondent for three different publications. I knit scarves, mittens, and hats and sewed clothes as Christmas gifts for my five children, and I bought most of their toys and books from second-hand shops.

Once I purchased a discounted flocked tree that had been miscolored a bright orange. (My children loved it.) Two of our best holidays were the times my family was selected to receive gifts provided by secret Santas.

To make ends meet, I canned fruit and vegetables (around 200 bottles each year) and made bread every week. I regret that I was too ashamed to apply for free school lunches for my children.

I understood the constraints that come in a patriarchal society. I was among many reporters who covered the short tenure of Utah's only female governor, Olene Walker, a beloved elected official with an astounding eighty-six percent approval rating.

Walker had won several terms as a legislator and made her mark in several leadership positions, including House majority whip. She was elected Utah's lieutenant governor as the running mate of Gov. Mike Leavitt in 1992. She became Utah's fifteenth governor in 2003 when Leavitt resigned after being named by President George W. Bush to head the Environmental Protection Agency.

Walker was no novice. She had been a proactive lieutenant governor for over a decade, instrumental in creating the Children's Health Insurance Program and consolidating employment, welfare, and other resources into a single department.

Her accomplishments outside government were also formidable. Walker was president of a food company. She earned a bachelor's, master's, and doctoral degree from Brigham Young University, Stanford, and the University of Utah respectively, making her, arguably, Utah's most educated governor.

Yet Walker was consistently referred to as a grandmother in the media, including *The Salt Lake Tribune*. For their part, reporters dutifully recorded chauvinistic comments from male politicians. One story quoted a male colleague saying Walker's grandmother image was something she had to overcome: "We think of grandmothers as not getting into fights and politics is a fight, it's a battle, and not all women can do it. Not all men can do it. What Olene has to accomplish is being tough without losing her femininity."

Another article reported that "reaching grandmother status and moving past menopause don't relegate a woman to a life of playing bingo at the senior center and booking cruises on the Princess Line."

These comments failed to convey Walker's abilities as a leader, reinforcing stereotypes based on candidates' gender. This was the conclusion of a study conducted by Utah State University, which looked at coverage of women candidates between 1995 and 2020. The analysis of the *Tribune*, *Deseret News*, and two other newspapers showed that one-third of articles describing women candidates emphasized their gender. Even when earlier coverage included gender, newspapers continued to harp about their sex. One article described a race between two female candidates, with a no-brainer observation that the winner "will be a woman."

I was infuriated with the media's treatment of Walker. I don't recall a time when male politicians were referred to as husbands, fathers, and grandfathers—unless they themselves mentioned their gender.

Still, I know of no reporter who didn't admire Walker. One reporter called the governor, "a nice lady," without understanding that the term is patronizing.

Despite her astounding approval rating, the highest in Utah history, she failed to win the gubernatorial election in her own right. Delegates rejected her in the Republican State Convention, denying her a place on the GOP primary ballot. The conservative delegates were cool to her push for more funding for education, despite that position's popularity with the general public. And the state's patriarchal culture made it difficult for delegates to accept a "grandma" as Utah's highest executive leader.

Politicians have long boasted that Utah was the first in the nation to have a woman cast a ballot. In 1920, twenty-three-year-old schoolteacher Seraph Young went to the polls in a municipal election, two days after the passage of the 19th Amendment to the U.S. Constitution, giving women the same suffrage rights as men.

Today, however, the Beehive State has been named the worst state

Seraph Young
Used by permission: Utah State Historical Society

for women. Utah ranks dead last when assessed on metrics measuring women's equality—for the fourth year in a row, according to a 2021 report from the personal finance website WalletHub. In 2022, Utah was again ranked as the worst state for women's equality—the fifth year in a row the state has ranked last in the annual analysis. The measurements include environment, education, health, and political empowerment.

The biggest difference between Utah and Idaho—the second worst state—is in political empowerment. The number of women elected to federal and state legislature and state executive jobs gave Utah a low score of 29.85 compared to Idaho's less dismal record of 37.37.

Now I worry for my granddaughters. Utah's wage and educational gap have dogged the state for decades. It still ranks near the bottom in wages paid to women when compared to men and numbers of women graduating from college. The state ranks 38th in the nation in both women's annual earnings and the wage gap when compared to their male counterparts and 30th in the nation in the percentage of women earning a bachelor's degree or higher. So, though more Utah girls are planning careers, they'll understand what inequality means when they cash their paychecks.

Worse, Utah women are more likely to suffer violence than their counterparts nationwide, according to the 2017 Utah Women & Leadership Project. One in three Utah women will suffer some form of domestic violence in their lifetime at a rate of 32.4 percent—versus 28.8 percent nationwide.

In addition, the Utah Domestic Violence Coalition reports that 40 percent of all adult homicides since 2000 have been domestic violence related. A recent report showed that 86 percent of Utah women believe domestic violence is a problem in their community and 63 percent said violence against women is increasing.

Sadly, the current plague suffered by women in modern times is symptomatic of the violence and lawlessness that ravaged the 19th-century frontier.

Front row left to right: Harry Alonzo Longabaugh, alias the Sundance Kid; Ben Kilpatrick, alias the Tall Texan; Robert Leroy Parker, alias Butch Cassidy. Back row left to right: Will Carver, alias News Carver; Harvey Logan, alias Kid Curry. Fort Worth, Texas, 1900.

CHAPTER TEN
Following God into Hell's Backbone

"In the latter half of the nineteenth century the Territory of Utah was a hotbed of two distinct cultural phenomena. One was religious. ... The other could be called irreligious: Utah appeared to be the center of the rise of the American outlaw, rustler, thief, gunfighter, bank robber, and hold-up man."

—TERRY ABRAHAM
professor, librarian, University of Idaho

George, Ethalinda, and their parents were a peaceful clan. But the families weren't immune to fronter violence ignited by religious zealots and cold-blooded killers.

Before moving to Poverty Flat, the Morrills and Ethalinda's parents helped resettle Circleville, which had been abandoned during the Black Hawk War. The war erupted in 1865 after a terrible winter had left tribes starving. Mormon pioneers had taken over hunting and fishing grounds. Settlers' livestock also competed for water, grasses, and open spaces. The Utes, led by Black Hawk, began driving off cattle and killing settlers. The Paiutes did not join in the raids as they were longtime enemies of the Utes, who made a practice of kidnapping Paiute women and children to be sold as slaves.

However, the distinction between tribes became blurred after seventy whites were killed in dozens of skirmishes and attacks. Frightened Circleville townspeople rounded up nearby Paiutes, disarmed them, and placed them under guard in town. When the Paiute men tried to escape, the settlers shot them down. The surviving men, women, and children were locked in a cellar. Soon, the townsfolk decided to silence all Paiute witnesses.

To save on ammunition, they slashed the Paiutes' throats, murdering some thirty of them. One Paiute mother had just enough time to tell her young daughter and two sons to run. The Circleville militia found the terrified youngsters hiding in a cave and took them to neighboring Marysville to see if they could be sold. When nobody wanted the girl, one man swung the child by her heels and bashed her head against a wagon wheel, cracking open her skull and killing her. Her brother was sold to a Mormon family in exchange for a horse and a bushel of wheat. There are no records of what happened to the third child.

It would be 150 years before a monument would be erected to honor the fallen people.[1] The inscription, written by Paiutes reads: "In remembrance of the innocent who were lost in this place so long ago. None of us could ever hope to describe the feelings of emotion that these people might have felt. All we can do is honor their existence as human beings."

The Circleville Massacre virtually wiped out the Koosharem band of the Paiutes. No investigation was conducted into the murders.

The Morrills and John and Margaret Young were resettling this troubled land in the 1870s at a time when more violence was rising. Unlike frontier outposts struggling along windswept flats and barren escarpments, Circleville seemed idyllic. The hamlet was nestled in a small, fertile valley, fed by the Sevier River and protected by a ring of

---

1. In 2016.

mountains. The lands surrounding Circleville are colorful, rugged, and dreamlike. But the majesty of the mountains did not make life easy. The area is remote, and many settlements could only support a few families. Some ranchers took to rustling cattle. It was easy to separate a calf from its mother, making it a maverick that could be claimed by anyone.

George Morrill's father, Laban, noted the settlement's lack of faith and community pride. "I had found the people in Circleville in a disinterested and lamentable condition, being many nationalities and opinions," he said. "Tho the little (Mormon) branch had been organized for 7 years, there was no school house, meeting house, or public building of any kind."

The Youngs' and Morrills' farms, on the outskirts of town, were almost next door to each other. Between them lived the Parkers, whose father, Maximillian Parker, fit Laban's description. He was a Mormon convert from England but had since lapsed and become what was known as a Jack Mormon. He did not wear the sacred undergarments given to Mormons after entering a temple. He likely smoked and drank alcohol, coffee, or tea. He had been alienated from the church after a local Mormon bishop awarded land he had homesteaded to a more righteous neighbor when Utah theocracy trumped secular rule. Maximillian passed along his grudge to his children.

There were twelve Parkers, surrounded by twenty-four Morrills and Youngs, according to the 1880 Census, in that tight-knit Mormon hamlet, with a population four hundred. Their children likely played together, perhaps a primitive form of baseball, using homemade balls of twine and a flat board for a bat. In neighboring Sevier County, baseball was so popular that Mormon wards fielded their own competitive teams.

The best-known Parker child was Robert Leroy Parker. He was thirteen years old in 1879 when his family moved from his birthplace of Beaver, Utah, over the Tushar Mountains to Circleville. Robert began skipping out on religious services and taking up with local outlaws. His father had sympathy for lawbreakers. The names of Robert, his father, and other family members were listed on a petition asking clemency for John D. Lee, convicted in the murder of white settlers passing through Utah. Their reasoning was that other men were "equally guilty of the crime," but only Lee had been convicted.[2]

After he left Circleville in 1884, Robert met an old drifter and rustler named Mike Cassidy who taught him to ride and shoot, soon introducing him to men living outside the law. As Robert started his criminal exploits, he did not want to embarrass his mother, who was still a churchgoing Mormon, so he took Mike's last name and then replaced Robert with Butch, supposedly from the time he spent working in a butcher shop. Thus, Butch Cassidy was born.[3]

Butch Cassidy became one of many outlaws who rustled cattle, robbed trains, and held up banks throughout the West. Early in his criminal career, Cassidy was imprisoned in Wyoming, but he won a pardon after promising the governor he would not break laws in that newly created state. It was a promise he kept while amassing a gang of horse thieves, cattle rustlers, and killers—dubbed the Wild Bunch. True to his word, Cassidy and his gang committed their crimes elsewhere.

Stories often cast Butch Cassidy as a frontier Robin Hood. He was careful to pay families for food and lodging while he was running from posses, making friends along the way who suffered convenient memory lapses when lawmen came around. Although Cassidy claimed he was

---

2. Bill Betenson, *Butch Cassidy, My Uncle* (Glendo, WY: High Plains Press, 2016), 30.

3. Though he had many other aliases, including Bud, Sally, Bob, George Cassidy, Mike Cassidy, George Low, Jim Lowe, Roy Parker, Santiago Maxwell, James Santiago Ryan, and Brady.

innocent of any murders, other members of the Wild Bunch killed several lawmen.

Cassidy, Harry Longabaugh (nicknamed the Sundance Kid), and the Wild Bunch robbed trains and banks in Utah, Colorado, New Mexico, Nevada, South Dakota, and Wyoming. The gang hid out along the Outlaw Trail, which is still difficult to reach today.

One of the outlaws' favorite hideaways was Hole-in-the-Wall, a remote pass located in Wyoming's Big Horn Mountains. They also fled to Robbers Roost in southeastern Utah and Brown's Park, a high mountain valley at the intersection of Utah, Wyoming, and Colorado.

The myth of lost gold surrounds Robbers Roost. Cassidy and his best friend, Elzy Lay,[4] robbed $7,000 from Pleasant Valley Coal Company in Castle Gate, Utah, before secreting the loot while heading to their hideout. The gold was supposedly never recovered, inspiring hikers since then to be on the lookout in the backcountry.

The undoing of the Wild Bunch came down to five of the men posing for a 1900 tintype, which fell into the hands of lawmen. Reward posters displayed their photographs, bringing in tips from around the West. In 1901, Detective William Pinkerton told *The Salt Lake Tribune*, "these hardened criminals have weak spots and one of the weakest spots in their nature is sitting for pictures." Gangs "simply got together, and after enjoying a visit felt so important that they could not resist the temptations of the camera."

The photograph, dubbing the Wild Bunch the Fort Worth Five, led to the capture of Kid Curry,[5] who died by his own hand in Colora-

---

4. Lay was eventually sentenced to life in prison after his 1899 arrest for a train robbery in New Mexico. In 1906 he helped stop a riot in the Territorial Prison and was granted a pardon. Elzy Lay operated a ranch and saloon in Wyoming, dug irrigation canals in Southern California, and in 1934 died in Los Angeles.

5. He was wanted for fifteen murders.

do; William Carver,[6] nicknamed News because he liked reading about his exploits; and Ben Kilpatrick, who was killed during a train robbery.

Cassidy and the Sundance Kid fled to South America. There, they might have been killed in a shootout or perhaps faked their deaths and returned to Utah. The *Salt Lake Herald-Republican* listed the many bogus reports of Cassidy's capture: He had been arrested in St. Louis, incarcerated in Nevada, killed after robbing a bank in Utah, and died again in Idaho. Posses captured him in Wyoming and Montana, and he was fatally shot numerous times in Arizona. Next, "we'll hear that M. Butch de Cassidy has been nabbed in sunny France or that Butchovitch Cassidowsky is in the hands of the czar's policeoff," noted the newspaper. "With Cassidy anything seems to be possible except really being caught."

Newspapers and modern films have romanticized the outlaws' exploits, but the fact is, his bank robberies ruined many farmers and ranchers. The federal government did not start insuring banks until the 1930s.

The outlaw's life was memorialized in the Academy Award-winning 1969 film, *Butch Cassidy and the Sundance Kid*, staring Paul Newman and Robert Redford. In 1981 Redford founded an arts institute named for Cassidy's accomplice. The Sundance Film Festival has since become the world's largest independent film event.

Cassidy's family home, located three miles south of Circleville on U.S. 89, is a tourist site, and each year, the Piute County Fair celebrates Butch Cassidy Days. The fair at the neighboring town of Junction features rodeos, movies, food, and races amid banners emblazoned with Cassidy's name.

Near the Morrills' home at Capitol Reef, steep inclines and switchbacks lead to Cassidy Arch, named for a nearby hiding place. Torrey

---

6. He was killed by Texas lawmen.

has its own apocryphal stories of Cassidy disappearing into rugged lands inside today's park. And old-timers refer to seedier elements who hung around Torrey as the Green River boys, which means anyone outside the law.[7]

Yet all the killings perpetrated by Cassidy's gang does not compare to the horrific mass murders and lasting heartache that George Morrill's father Laban risked his life to stop.

---

7. One of Cassidy's cohorts, Silver Tip Hawkins (nicknamed for streaks of grey hair) was captured by Torrey Sheriff John A. Hancock. The cattle rustler and horse thief had been imprisoned on charges of attempted murder after an 1899 shootout near Robbers Roost. He escaped until Hancock (who became sheriff at age 18) tracked him down. Hancock waited until the outlaw was out for a walk to make the arrest. Accounts of Hawkins's final days vary—much as Cassidy's do—but he escaped again and was either killed in a shootout in Arizona or lived a quiet life in Wyoming.

Laban Morrill

CHAPTER ELEVEN
A Blacksmith Who Tried to Stop a Massacre

"Yet, from the darkness of moral blindness and bigotry of Mormonism, the personality of Laban Morrill rises like a shaft of light and serves notice to the world that there are Mormons who are infinitely better than their religion."

—JOSIAH FRANCIS GIBBS
newspaper reporter, 1917

On the day George Morrill was born (September 18, 1857, in Cedar City), the stench of death hung over a dell fifty miles away where 125 men, women, and children had been slaughtered the week before in an atrocity known as the Mountain Meadows Massacre. George's father, Laban Morrill, was the man who tried to stop it.

Laban was a devout Mormon who suffered mightily for his faith. He had converted to the Mormon Church twenty-four years earlier at age nineteen, an act that prompted his parents to disown him. He moved with the Saints to Far West, Missouri, and built a home. But mobs soon destroyed the LDS colony and drove them out of the state. Laban, his wife, and three young children fled to the Mormon city of Nauvoo in Illinois.

But only Laban survived the fevers that plagued the swampy area.

After LDS Church founder, Joseph Smith, was martyred, the bereft Laban joined the exodus across the Plains to little-known lands in the Great Basin Desert.

Yet while the first pioneers were entering Salt Lake Valley in 1847, Laban had stayed behind to help other Mormons outfit their wagons and horses to cross the Plains. He finally arrived in 1852 after the choicest lands and perpetual water rights had been claimed. So he set up a blacksmith shop in Springville and helped construct several buildings, including a dance hall.

Laban had a commanding physical presence, standing six feet tall and weighing two hundred pounds. Years of heavy labor in the Western wildlands had made him strong and unafraid.

On September 6, 1857, twelve days before George was born, Laban was stunned to hear some Mormons openly discussing a plot to kill emigrants in the Baker-Fancher wagon train, from Arkansas, then passing through southern Utah. The conspirators told him rumors that the emigrants had been heard to brag about killing Joseph Smith and raping Mormon women as they drove the Saints from their homes. They claimed that men in the wagon train had poisoned springs along the route in Utah and threatened to kill every damn Mormon.

To add fuel to the fire, LDS Church leaders had warned that the U.S. Army was marching to Utah to annihilate the Mormons and replace Brigham Young as governor, so obedience to the church had become paramount. LDS scholars say that a dangerous concentration of civil, religious, and military power was in the hands of a few local church leaders, while "impoverished settlers knew the value of obeying."[1]

Inflaming feelings even more were memories of persecutions the

1. Ron W. Walker, Richard E. Turley Jr. and Glen M. Leonard, *Massacre at Mountain Meadows* (New York: Oxford University Press, 2011), 127–128.

Mormons in southern Utah had suffered before journeying to Utah Territory. Some had survived the 1838 mob attack at Haun's Mill, Missouri, or they had known someone among the thirty-two Mormons who had been wounded or killed.

Though Laban Morrill had endured these early persecutions, and though he had no reason to doubt the rumors surrounding the wagon train camped outside Cedar City, he also believed in the teachings of his Savior. This became evident at a September 6 meeting where local leaders were discussing what to do about the emigrants. Laban stood up to speak. "Do not our principles of right teach us to return good for evil and do good to those who despitefully use us?" he remembered asking. "To fall upon them and destroy them was the work of savage monsters rather than that of civilized beings of our own enlightened time."

Laban Morrill proposed that they send a rider 250 miles north to Salt Lake City to get instructions from Brigham Young before the Mormon militia made any kind of move against the wagon train. "I persuaded them to wait till I could get a message to Governor Young which they promised to do," he later wrote. As Laban sat down, he spotted two men, William Stewart and Daniel Macfarlane, slipping out of the meeting. Fearing they would ambush him, Laban altered his route and hurried to his home at Fort Johnson, outside Cedar City.

The rider, James Haslam, mounted his horse the following day and galloped off to church headquarters. Haslam was a block of a man who had been appointed Iron County sheriff in 1853 and later would ride for the Pony Express. He carried a letter from his local church leaders directing bishops along his route to provide him with fresh mounts.

Some bishops were reluctant to give up good horses for this grueling endurance run, so Haslam sometimes wasted time pleading for a mount. In one instance, he had to wait for a bishop to return from hunting. Riding mustangs, workhorses, and unbroken broncos, he went sixteen hours without rest. Haslam was so exhausted at one point that he fell asleep on a bishop's porch. The bishop returned in an hour, splashed cold water in Haslam's face, and handed him a cup of strong coffee. A fresh horse was saddled up and ready to go. In the final push to Salt Lake City, Haslam rode overnight.

In a little more than three days, Haslam made his way to Brigham Young. He was told to rest, eat, and return in an hour, whereupon he was given a letter telling the militia to let the emigrants go in peace.[2] But even with a letter from the prophet himself, Haslam still had difficulty getting fresh horses on his return trip. Seventy hours later, an exhausted Haslam delivered the prophet's answer to Mormon leader Isaac Haight. Haight sobbed uncontrollably after reading the letter, managing only to say, "Too late, too late."

The day Haslam had left, September 7, 1857, Mormon militiamen (some dressed as American Indians) and a few Southern Paiutes surrounded the Baker-Fancher wagon train. On Friday, September 11, the attacks began.[3]

One of the men Laban had feared would ambush him, William Stewart, came upon an emigrant, William Aden, who was looking for

---

2. Some historians say Brigham Young supported the massacre but dared not put a killing order in writing. As Will Bagley wrote, "Like many great crimes of power, the criminals expected to get away with it…Even if he burned every incriminating piece of evidence and persuaded every believing resident in Utah Territory to swear that he had nothing to do with the horror at Mountain Meadows, Brigham Young could not change the past. He knew the full truth of his complicity in the crime." Will Bagley, *Blood of the Prophets: Brigham Young and the Massacre at Mountain Meadows, 380.*

3. The date is a horrific coincidence to another attack on Sept. 11, 2001, when an Islamic group of Al Qaeda terrorists crashed four highjacked planes, killing more than 3,000 people in New York City, rural Pennsylvania, and the Pentagon in Washington, D.C.

cattle that had strayed from the wagon train. Pausing at a stream, Stewart asked Aden if he could borrow a tin cup to get himself a drink. When Aden reached for the cup attached to the back of his saddle, Stewart shot the man through the head, instantly killing him.[4]

Meanwhile, some Southern Paiute Indians began firing on the wagon train, but well-armed sharpshooters fought off the Paiutes, prompting the Mormon militia to step in. The Mormons tricked the emigrants into giving up their guns by promising to escort them to safety. The other man Laban was worried about, Daniel Macfarlane, led a roundup of women and children and was tasked with capturing anyone trying to escape. The unarmed men, each flanked by a Mormon soldier, were executed at close range. Stewart became so frenzied in the killing spree that he broke from the ranks to kill men who survived the first volley of bullets. The militia then turned on the women and children, slitting their throats or hacking them to death. Only seventeen small children, thought to be too young to remember, were spared.[5]

"God forbid that the pages of my journal should be strained with the recital of a crime so foul," Laban wrote. "But I want my children's children to know that sin like this is, and has ever been, loathed by me and is in direct opposition to the teachings of our Father."

What we know of the plot to attack the emigrants comes primarily from the testimony of Laban Morrill during a trial held nearly twenty

---

4. Aden, 19, was a poet, adventurer, and had recently joined the wagon train. Aden's father, who earlier had befriended a Mormon missionary in Tennessee, spent years vainly searching for his missing son.

5. Two years after the massacre, U.S. Army troops escorted the orphans back to Arkansas. Sarah Dunlap—whose sister found her in the arms of their dead mother—faced a dismal future. Bullets had torn through her right arm, rendering it useless. She had also contracted an eye disease in Utah that left her partially blind. One of the soldiers, Capt. John Lynch, married her in 1893. He was 74. She was 38. Lynch liked to tell how he rescued her from the Mormons.

years later, in 1876. Laban testified that the most difficult man he dealt with was Philip Klingensmith, who used his influence as a bishop to help plan the mass murder. Klingensmith admitted to murdering one or two emigrants before the massacre and had ordered at least one of the surviving children killed. But during the first trial, jurors, primarily made up of Mormons, could not reach a verdict.

LDS scholars blame Klingensmith, John D. Lee, and other local leaders for the mass killings. "Many of the men who went to the Meadows were militia officers or had attended Sunday's council in which the emigrants' destruction was proposed. Most likely these men saw the euphemisms and untruths for what they were and only later claimed to be unaware of their true meaning. In crime, the first casualty is often truth," three scholars wrote in *Massacre at Mountain Meadows*.[6]

John D. Lee was the only person convicted of murder in connection with the massacre.[7] On March 23, 1877, federal troops took him to the site where the emigrants had been slaughtered and executed him by firing squad. According to an 1877 account, *The Salt Lake Tribune* reported that just before his death, Lee made conflicting statements to various people. To some he admitted taking part in the killing, but to others he denied his guilt altogether. Publicly, Lee insisted he was a scapegoat—a sacrifice to appease national outcries against the horrific killings. "I have been sacrificed in a cowardly and dastardly manner," Lee declared. As the firing squad took aim, he sat in his coffin and told his executioners to "aim well."[8]

---

6. Ron W. Walker, Richard E. Turley Jr. and Glen M. Leonard, *Massacre at Mountain Meadows*, 180.

7. John D. Lee led the first attack on the wagon train and reportedly admitted murdering five or six emigrants. Walker, Turley, and Leonard, *Massacre at Mountain Meadows*, 230–31.

8. The descendants of John D. Lee have long maintained that he was not among the

John D. Lee
Courtesy: Church History Library, Salt Lake City

For years, body parts, hair, and patches of clothing were found in Mountain Meadows. Fear, disgust, and a general economic collapse in Iron County caused many families to move away. Two years after the massacre, less than half the families remained in Cedar City. James Haslam, the man who made the ride to Salt Lake City and back, was among the people who relocated. Laban Morrill, troubled at the stain

conspirators and had not killed anyone. Lee's fate was sealed after Brigham Young excommunicated him for extreme wickedness, which led to his execution. In 1961 the LDS Church posthumously restored Lee's membership. The First Presidency and Council of Twelve Apostles said in a statement: "It was the action of the Council after considering all the facts available that authorization be given for the reinstatement to membership and former blessings to John D. Lee."

on the land, purchased a small farm at Circleville "and prepared to leave Iron County permanently." In all, he had helped settle some twenty frontier hamlets in five counties spanning 260 miles. Many relocations were assignments from Mormon leaders, who desperately needed tradesmen to open new settlements. In the late 1860s, Church authorities called him to Springdale to help establish a short-lived co-operative called the United Order.

While living in Springdale, today's gateway city to Zion National Park, Laban took a third plural wife, a widow named Mary Behunin.[9] He was 55 years old; she was thirty with four children. Laban was father to fourteen at the time. But the marriage began to sour in 1869, Laban writing, "We separated finding that the differences of feeling which existed between us was not productive of happiness."

That "difference of feeling" was probably Laban's expectations of wifely obedience and Mary's rebellion against it. He told his children how he decided to marry his first wife, Loraine, before moving west. He met several young women who he said agreed that he could take his pick of them to wed. When he announced to the women that he needed a button sewn on his trousers, "Loraine was the one who got busy and did the job."

Less than three months after Loraine died, Laban married the woman who would become George Morrill's mother, Permelia Drury. Laban paid tribute to her, saying, "Never has thou murmured or complained." Laban also praised another wife, Lydia Davis, for her compliance and devotion.

In 1885, when Laban was seventy-two years old, federal officials charged him with bigamy, a crime that could have sent him to prison. He pleaded guilty, promised to obey all laws, and divorced Lydia, his

9. Daughter-in-law to Isaac Behunin, who is credited with giving the Zion National Park area its name. Overwhelmed by its beauty, he told friends, "A man can worship God among these great cathedrals as well as he can in any man-made church; this is Zion."

plural wife of thirty-one years. The non-Mormon judge granted leniency because of Laban's advanced age and his long-ago efforts to stop the massacre at Mountain Meadows.

There is no record of the gentle Lydia complaining of her husband's choice to leave her. He and her former sister-wife Permelia frequently visited her, and Laban continued to refer to her as his wife.

In 1892, Laban and Permelia were returning home after seeing Lydia when their cart overturned. Permelia was thrown against a wheel and suffered internal injuries. She died that night at age seventy-one. Laban wrote of his grief: "Now thou art gone and I am left behind / Lonely and cast down."

The following year, Lydia died at age sixty. A daughter wrote of her: "She was willing to sacrifice her own pleasure, if by so doing she could make others happy."

When Laban was seventy-eight years old, he was alone and slowly going blind.[10] The giant man, accustomed to arduous labors, became helpless. He relied on his grandchildren to lead him to places he needed to go. He moved in with a son whose brother lived across the street. His two sons stretched a wire across Main Street and attached it to two trees, allowing Laban to use a long stick with a loop attached to guide him between the two homes.

According to Laban's daughter Sarah, he had helped "build schools and meeting houses, planting shade trees and orchards, building bridges, making fences, doing something to improve the country." Laban now tended the garden, feeling his way to weed and pick off bugs from berry bushes. He dictated his life story to a son, waited for someone to read aloud the newspaper, and prayed his sight would return. Some of his vision did return during the last five months of his life, enabling him to distinguish people he knew and to walk about town unaided.

---

10. His children believed his blindness was caused because of cataracts.

On December 8, 1891—his birthday—Laban fell from his horse and was given a blessing that he would live. When he regained consciousness, he asked, "Why didn't you let me go?" While he was recovering, however, Laban heard a voice promising he would live nine years longer. Laban Morrill died on his birthday, December 8, 1900. He was eighty-six.

The *Deseret News* and its rival, *The Salt Lake Tribune*, called Laban a man of sterling character and one of the most widely known men in southern Utah. The *Tribune* called him a hero for trying to stop the Mountain Meadows Massacre. The church-owned *Deseret News* made no mention of the murders.

The Mountain Meadows Massacre is rarely discussed at church gatherings and Laban Morrill is therefore virtually unknown. Because Laban failed to stop the killings, he is only briefly mentioned in several books describing the darkest history of the Mormon Church. Laban's descendants, however, know of his compassion for perceived enemies as well his devotion to his church. Despite John D. Lee's claims of innocence, Laban Morrill blamed Lee for his role in the conspiracy and killings.[11]

In a strange and unforeseen twist, we discovered the Mountain Meadows Massacre continues to be a political minefield in modern-day Utah. *The Salt Lake Tribune* became embroiled in the controversy, which led to a series of events that resulted in my husband's resignation from the newspaper where he had worked for more than forty years.

---

11. The connection to Mountain Meadows came up in 2010 when Mike Lee, a direct descendant to John D. Lee, successfully ran for the U.S. Senate. His Democratic opponent was Sam Granato, whose ancestor was severely beaten by neighbors after giving vegetables to a doomed settler. Mike Lee is known as a conservative ideologue. His father, Rex Lee, served as President Ronald Reagan's solicitor general.

Cairn at Mountain Meadows Massacre Site
Credit: Mangoman88

CHAPTER TWELVE
The Haunting of Mountain Meadows

"The Salt Lake Daily and Weekly Tribune *are the only newspapers published in Salt Lake City independent of (LDS) Church control."*

—J. Cecil Alter
Early Utah Journalism

The Mountain Meadows Massacre has haunted Utah and Mormon history for more than a century. Its shadow has even dogged Utah's largest daily newspaper.

Founded in 1871 by excommunicated Mormons, *The Salt Lake Tribune* soon engaged the LDS Church, and, by extension, the *Deseret News*, in a protracted culture war. While Ethalinda Morrill was taking fanciful worldwide journeys through *Comfort* magazine, insulating her barren cabin with them when she was finished, the *Tribune* and *Deseret News* were duking it out in Salt Lake City. The two state-wide newspapers created an atmosphere of hate that resembled the bitter climate leading to the Mountain Meadows Massacre a generation earlier.

It was the era of yellow journalism; facts and objectivity giving way to opinion, slander, and hyperbole in both newspapers. At the *Tribune*, objectivity "was a vice not to be tolerated in news columns, editorials or correspondence from readers," wrote O.N. Malmquist in *The First*

100 Years, A History of The Salt Lake Tribune 1871–1971. "The news columns and correspondence were frequently more opinionated than the editorials, possibly because the reporters and correspondents were more opinionated than the editorial writers."

The *Tribune's* attacks on the LDS Church and its leader Brigham Young elicited matching vitriolic responses from the *Deseret News.* For example, on August 29, 1877, when Brigham Young died, the *Tribune* opined that Young's despotism was unequaled globally, excepting the "barbarous" country of Turkey. "His death is regarded as the fall of a great man in Israel, and thousands mourn his loss as a personal bereavement. Yet we believe the most graceful act of his life has been his death."

The *Deseret News* called the *Tribune,* "the scavengers of the press; the slanderers of the living and defamers of the dead; the garblers of public speeches; the blasphemers of sacred things; the cowardly libelers of women and children; the dirty-minded scandal mongers; the craven dastards who fling their filth at those they know will not retaliate; the pen-stabbers; the character assassins; the authors of false telegraphic dispatches."

Despite this early rancor, the feud dwindled into an era of tranquility by the 1920s when the *Tribune's* then-publisher, John Fitzpatrick, and his successor, John W. "Jack" Gallivan, concluded that it would help the state economically if both sides would stop attacking each other.

Gallivan spent a lifetime finding common ground between the competing cultures and forged a deep friendship with the Mormon prophet David O. McKay, even though the *Tribune's* editorial pages often took positions opposite from the church and the *Deseret News.* For example, the *Tribune* advocated individual servings of alcohol at restaurants (liquor-by-the-drink) rather than patrons having to bring their own bottles to the tables, contrasting the Church's distrust of alcoholic drinks. Gallivan once joked, "If you want to get something defeated, just get the *Salt Lake Tribune* to endorse it."

But even with the editorial skirmishes between the *Tribune* and *Deseret News*, Gallivan's disarming style and kindness toward his opponents made him beloved among Mormons and non-Mormons alike. He was so revered that a square in downtown Salt Lake City was named the Gallivan Center in his honor.

Gallivan's best-known effort was his push in the 1960s to bring the Olympics to Utah. He lobbied then-governor Calvin Rampton to back him, but Rampton believed the state wasn't ready to build the world-class venues the games required. Over a shared bottle of Jack Daniels, the governor said he would back the 1966 bid only if Gallivan promised Utah would lose. But Gallivan's effort inspired a movement to prepare the state to be a potential host for a future Winter Olympics. The Utah Legislature passed a sales tax dedicated to building the infrastructure needed for the event. Many years later, the International Olympic Committee selected the Beehive State to host the 2002 Winter Games.

Despite Gallivan's dedication to advancing the state's economic prospects, some Mormon leaders never stopped suspecting the *Tribune* was anti-Mormon. And the peace he had brokered was shattered during the early 21st century with the resurrection of Mountain Meadows. It would cause the *Tribune* to lose its status as the state's leading news voice and push the newspaper out of its family's hands after nearly one hundred years of ownership.

The transformation began with a controversial series triggered by an incident on September 11, 1999—the 142nd anniversary of the massacre—when LDS Church president Gordon B. Hinckley rededicated the site of the killings. He had earlier visited the site and found it in such disrepair that he vowed to restore the monument to show respect to the victims. During the restoration process some thirty pounds of bones were uncovered. They had been overlooked by a contingent of U.S. Army soldiers who gathered and buried the victims' scattered remains two years after the attack.

Six months after the rededication ceremony, the first installment of a *Tribune* series on the massacre appeared on March 12, 2000. "When a backhoe operator last summer accidentally dug up the bones buried here in 1859 by (U.S. Maj. James) Carleton's troops, it set into motion a series of cover-ups, accusations and recriminations that continue today," it read. "It also caused a good-faith effort by The Church of Jesus Christ of Latter-day Saints—to reconcile one of the ugliest chapters of U.S. history—to backfire." One story described Mountain Meadows as "the Bermuda Triangle of Utah's historical and theological landscape."

Gallivan told Paul and me before his death in 2012 that he was shocked when he opened this issue of his paper. The *Tribune* "covered the massacre as if it had happened yesterday" and gave the story more play than the moon landing or the close of World War II. He knew this detailed account of the long-ago atrocities would reopen the rift he had worked for decades to heal between the Mormon Church and his newspaper.

Initially, *Deseret News* board chairman Glen Snarr and top Mormon leaders discussed taking over the *Tribune*. They even talked about the changes they would make in the newspaper's editorial content. Snarr suggested retaining *Tribune* editor Jay Shelledy—a Catholic—to make it appear that the publication would not be a Mormon newspaper, court filings show.

Relations between the newspapers grew complicated. Dominic Welch, *Tribune* publisher from 1994 to 2002, was viewed as unfriendly to the *Deseret News*. He had been the general manager of the Newspaper Agency Corp., which handled the business side of both newspapers, including circulation, advertising, and production. The company was managed by a board made up of *Tribune* and *Deseret News* executives. Welch was seen as resisting changes that would have boosted the *Deseret News'* circulation, such as moving it from an afternoon to a morning newspaper to compete with the much larger *Tribune*.

The *Deseret News* got its chance at a hostile takeover when *Tribune* owners agreed to a company stock transfer to cable television giant TCI, making that firm the newspaper's effective owner. One reason for the stock transfer was to avoid inheritance taxes, and the 1997 deal was a windfall for the heirs. The *Tribune*'s owners thought they had covered their bases by stipulating that they could buy the paper back in five years, but TCI merged with AT&T, which challenged the validity of the stock deal—including the clause allowing the former *Tribune* owners to buy back the newspaper.

The merger left the *Tribune* exposed to potential outside buyers, opening the way for Mormon leaders to make their move. It was eventually decided that the LDS Church couldn't buy the *Tribune* because of public-image and antitrust issues. Instead, Church leaders backed a bidder named Dean Singleton, owner of a chain of newspapers called Media News Group, which was seen as friendly to the Mormon Church.

The McCarthey family, *Tribune* heirs and majority stockholders, fought a lengthy and expensive legal battle, which cost the contenders a combined $60 million. The *Deseret News* had gotten considerable help from Utah political leaders, many of whom were Mormons. The family became frustrated when Utah judges consistently ruled against them in complicated legal motions, but they were encouraged to continue the legal fight after an appeals court in Denver overturned the lower courts' rulings. The continued battle, however, cost the McCartheys more money. The family finally settled, and Singleton took over *The Salt Lake Tribune*.

The takeover proved costly. Singleton operated his newspaper chain under the weight of enormous debt, which increased substantially with the purchase of the *Tribune*. When the Great Recession hit in 2008, Singleton reacted to continuing pressures on the print news business imposed by the rise of the Internet by selling the significant interests in his newspaper chain to the banks that were his creditors. In 2013, the banks, in turn, sold the *Tribune* to a New York hedge fund, whose interests were not to preserve the newspaper but to sell off its parts and make a profit for its shareholders.

The *Deseret News* seized the opportunity to control the *Tribune*, paying Alden Global Capital LLC $25 million in exchange for control of the printing presses and a change in the makeup of the old NAC company, renamed MediaOne.

Now the *Deseret News* controlled the board and revenues. The *Tribune* always enjoyed a 58-42 percent revenue split, reflecting its more extensive circulation, but the revenue split was changed to 70-30 in favor of the *Deseret News*. It was only a matter of time before the *Tribune* would go out of business.

Joan O'Brien (daughter of the late *Tribune* publisher Jerry O'Brien), former staffers, and other stakeholders formed a group to legally challenge the new revenue split and the *Deseret News*' absolute veto power over ownership of the *Tribune*.

For years, billionaire Jon Huntsman Sr. had considered taking ownership of the *Tribune*. Huntsman planned to use his deep pockets to sustain the financially bleeding newspaper until it could be stabilized. His son, Paul Huntsman, purchased the *Tribune* in 2016 but quickly grew tired of losing hundreds of thousands of dollars each month. After his father died in 2018, he laid off a third of the staff and cut the size of the daily newspaper considerably. In his speech to *Tribune* staffers before the layoffs, Paul Huntsman recounted his financial losses, justifying the firings in part because he had to send his children to college. Six *Tribune* veterans, including my husband, Paul Rolly, resigned to save younger employees' jobs.

In 2016 Paul Huntsman fired editor/publisher Terry Orme, who had been instrumental in a *Tribune* series examining a coverup of college rapes that won the paper a 2017 Pulitzer Prize. Huntsman also converted the *Tribune* into a nonprofit enterprise. The *Tribune* now accepts tax-deductible donations to help with operation costs.

The Mountain Meadows Massacre's deep influence on the *Salt Lake Tribune* reminded me of a thought recorded by historian John Gary Maxwell: "This pivotal chapter in the history book of the Utah Territory and the Mormons remains open and unfinished."

The state's legacy of strict patriarchy, extremism, and zealotry also remains open and unfinished.

CHAPTER THIRTEEN
Murders Most Mormon

"Ambiguity vanishes from the fanatic's worldview; a narcissistic sense of self-assurance displaces all doubt. A delicious rage quickens his pulse, fueled by the sins and shortcomings of lesser mortals, who are soiling the world wherever he looks."

—JOHN KRAKAUER
Under the Banner of Heaven: A Story of Violent Faith

While Ethalinda married a lawbreaker, I made a career of covering their misdeeds for *The Salt Lake Tribune*. My research about criminals in the Utah Territory brought memories of my own brushes with some of the state's most notorious sinners one hundred years later. Many of the criminals I covered were violent, religious zealots.

My first encounter with a cold-blooded killer was Ron Lafferty. He lived down the street from my home in Highland, thirty miles south of Salt Lake City. My family worshiped with Lafferty and his family. We went on a camping trip together, and his six children attended the same religious classes and elementary school my five children attended.

I began writing stories about Ron Lafferty shortly after he was elected to Highland's founding city council in 1977. He ran on the promise of keeping the town safe, family friendly, and, above all, rural.

One of his stated reasons for incorporating was to stop beer sales at a small country store. He was instrumental in turning down a grant that would have paid for sidewalks on State Road 92, the main thoroughfare through Highland. He worried that children would sneak out of their neighborhoods and get into trouble. (Sidewalks were installed years later.)

Ron's views went haywire sometime in the early 1980s. He ignored speeding tickets, which he maintained were unlawful. One evening he appeared at my door to object to my reports on court proceedings against him. He insisted that it was my duty to write about his sacred quest to save the U.S. Constitution.

I had known Ron for years, but while he stood at my door he seemed strangely menacing. When I explained that I wouldn't be covering his opinions outside of what he said in court, I could see him trying to control his rage. I telephoned the Mormon stake president (similar to a Catholic bishop) to warn him that Ron might be dangerous.

Not long after my telephone call, in 1984, Ron and his brother Dan Lafferty beat their sister-in-law Brenda Lafferty to death as she pleaded for the life of her 15-month-old daughter. Dan slit the baby's throat, which he told a couple of drifters was "no big deal." The Laffertys had decided that Brenda had to die for encouraging their wives to resist their fanaticism. Covered with blood, the two men drove to the stake president's house to kill him, too. Next on their list was a woman church leader from the same congregation who had been assisting Ron's wife as she prepared to leave him. But the Laffertys discovered that neither of their marks was in town.

Before Ron became a killer, he didn't seem much different from many of the men I knew in the community. He was rock hard in his understanding of the world, dismissive of women, and certain of his God-given Mormon priesthood authority over his wife and children.

Two different sentencing juries decided the Lafferty brothers' fates. Dan was sentenced to life in prison while Ron was sentenced to death—for essentially the same crime. After repeated, lengthy appeals, Ron died of natural causes.

Ron Lafferty's burgeoning evil frightened me. But the absolute depravity of forger/bomber Mark Hofmann gave me nightmares. He wasn't a religious zealot, but he preyed upon believers devoted to protecting their beloved church.

Hofmann was a self-professed historian who made the news by "discovering" original historical documents, often connected to the Mormon Church. Amateur documents collector Steve Christensen became suspicious of Hofmann's claims that he had discovered historical papers, known as the McLellin documents, that would prove embarrassing to the Mormon Church. The collection contained papers written by early Mormon apostle William McLellin, who left the Mormon Church over differences with its founder, Joseph Smith. Christensen demanded that Hofmann produce the documents on October 15, 1985, or face exposure as a fraud.

That morning, Hofmann placed a homemade pipe bomb filled with nails in the hallway of Christensen's Salt Lake City office. When Christensen picked it up, the package exploded in his hands, killing him.

Hofmann then placed a second bomb outside the home of Christensen's business partner, Gary Sheets, hoping it would steer police to investigate disgruntled clients who had invested in Christensen and Sheets' business ventures. Sheets' wife picked the package up on their driveway and was instantly killed. He later said his diversionary plot was like a game. He didn't care who picked up the bomb, "My thoughts were that it didn't matter if it was Mrs. Sheets, a child, a dog … whoever."

I had interviewed Mark Hofmann several times about his historical discoveries—including the McLellin Collection—before he became a killer to cover up his counterfeiting scheme. I started searching for the collection after Hofmann injured himself when a pipe bomb in his car detonated, making him a suspect.

Whenever I do research, I avoid assumptions and start from the last known fact. I knew that in 1901 a devotee of McLellin's had written to Mormon leaders, attempting to sell the late apostle's journals and personal papers. Hofmann also knew about the letter, which a graduate student came across in the New York Public Library. Hofmann conned wealthy investors wanting to protect the Mormon Church's reputation by telling them he needed cash to buy the collection, which, if made public, would cast doubt on the church's divine origins. A Mormon official, in turn, arranged a $185,000 signature loan for Hofmann to buy the documents.

I also knew from the address on the 1901 letter that the devotee, John Traughber, lived in a small town in Texas. From there, I used census records to plot towns where he, his widow, and their children lived, and marriage records to determine names of spouses. Using court documents, voter rolls, and telephone directories, I called surviving family members, asking if they knew about the collection. They did. In fact, their elder brother had locked the collection in a safety box. But they said Hofmann had never contacted them, indicating that Hofmann never had the papers.

Shortly after I located the collection in 1986, University of Utah officials flew to Texas to buy the documents. But the family patriarch, Otis Traughber, was in no hurry to sell since the collection had been in his family for nearly a century. Undaunted, assistant librarian Stan Larson began a correspondence with Traughber that lasted a decade. In 1996, the university purchased the documents for $15,000 with money from an anonymous donor.

Hofmann confessed to murder and forgery in 1986 and is serving a life sentence at the Utah State Prison.

I reported on a different kind of criminal in 1998, spawned from distorted interpretations of Mormon patriarchy. A polygamous father in the Kingston clan severely beat his sixteen-year-old daughter for running away to escape a forced marriage to her uncle.

After newspaper stories appeared about the injured girl walking miles to get help from strangers, I confronted her father. The only way I could find him was to wait until services ended at his church. In view of dozens of congregants, I asked why he beat his daughter. Our conservation turned into a shouting match. He was so enraged that without witnesses—including a *Tribune* photographer—I believe he might have attacked me.

I also reported on the Kingston polygamous clan's ties to an energy renewal plant. In 2019 two company executives pleaded guilty in what prosecutors said was a $511 million tax credit scheme.

I reported on another polygamous sect's reliance on government subsidies. We heard stories of possible welfare abuses involving a clan headed by the now-jailed Warren Jeffs. Because welfare rolls are private, I focused on the polygamous community living in the twin towns of Hildale, Utah, and Colorado City in Arizona. Members lived on land owned by the Fundamentalist Church of Jesus Christ of Latter Day Saints, making it easy to compare zip codes because nonmembers didn't live in the twin cities.

We compared the number of welfare recipients to towns and cities across the Intermountain West. Our research showed the polygamous twin cities collected considerably more government benefits than most other communities. When a photographer and I traveled to Hildale to question the town spokesman, I assured my colleague that unlike reports from other outsiders, an intimidating truckload of men and boys would not follow us as we drove into town. I was wrong. Even though the interview had been approved by church leaders, we were still tailgated.

Earlier, I investigated the clan's involvement in manufacturing O-rings for the space shuttle Challenger that exploded in 1986, killing all seven astronauts. The disaster was caused by the failure of two O-ring seals in the shuttle's solid rocket booster. Record-low temperatures during the launch prevented the rubber O-rings from sealing the joints, igniting a fire. When I asked FLDS Church leader Warren Jeffs about his father Rulon, who was president of the company that made

Utah State Penitentiary, 1903.
Used by permission: Utah State Historical Society

the O-rings, he began shouting at me. Even though the manufacturer was not faulted in the explosion, he called me a liar and threatened to sue. Jeffs terminated our phone interview when I referred him to the company's incorporation papers listing Rulon Jeffs as company president. The incorporation papers were changed the next day.

For a long time, I received repeated late-night hang-up calls at my home.

Warren Jeffs demanded complete obedience from his FLDS followers, and my experience showed he could not tolerate anyone questioning his authority. The clan eventually moved many of its members to Texas, where Jeffs was imprisoned for having sex with two underage girls he claimed as wives. One of the victims was twelve years old. He continues to direct church members from his prison cell.

As a veteran reporter and editor, I also covered conflicts of interests in local and state government. The Utah prison—where my brothers Tom and Fred House spent their careers —is one example. When the Draper prison opened in 1951, it replaced the old Territorial Penitentiary, where William Phelps and John D. Lee had been jailed.

During Phelps and Lee's incarcerations, the Penitentiary was underfunded and in disrepair. The compound consisted of the warden's house, a log structure that served as a dining room and meeting hall, a workshop and two cell houses filled with bunk beds. The facility looked something akin to a primitive castle. The walls of an outer court were made of adobe, twelve feet high and four feet thick, built upon a foundation of rock laid in lime mortar. Atop the wall was a boardwalk with wooden hand railings and four watchtowers at each corner. Sixteen cells made of iron bars were built underground.[1]

When the old Penitentiary closed, the state turned its grounds into

---

1. Escapes were rampant at the old Territorial Prison. From 1855 when the prison opened until 1878, about twenty-five percent of all inmates—from a total of some 240 men—escaped. Territorial Warden James A. Little was particularly unlucky. He left no record on the number of inmates in 1861, but every prisoner in his charge escaped except one. And he was pardoned. James B. Hill, "History of Utah State Prison 1850-1952" (master's thesis: Brigham Young University, 1952), 80–85.

a spacious public park. A high school also was built on the property in the Sugar House neighborhood of Salt Lake City. But the Draper prison that replaced it had become outdated and was slated for demolition.

A new facility was built in Salt Lake City, despite a study showing the cost of relocating the prison far exceeded its value from the sale of the property. In 2015, however, the Utah Legislature voted to move the state prison to wetlands, just west of the Salt Lake International Airport.

The state touted the Draper prison grounds as an economic engine, complete with housing and commercial development. But when the relocation commission announced several possible sites for the new penitentiary, none of the prospective communities wanted it.

After numerous secret meetings between legislative leaders and other stakeholders, the Draper prison property was sold to private developers and turned into a behemoth multipurpose commercial metropolis. It may be no coincidence that several legislators involved in the decision-making process are real-estate agents and developers. The prison opened in 2022. Costs escalated to $1 billion (double the official estimate), which included battling sinking soil in the surrounding wetlands and developing habitats for migratory birds.

It is probably no accident that the new prison was placed in Salt Lake City, which, in contrast to the rest of the state, has a majority of Democrats whose influence has been diluted through gerrymandering. The partisan tactic has weakened Democrats' leverage as Republican lawmakers have dissected voting districts to ensure a GOP advantage.

Before our retirement, my husband and I often took breaks from our work to relax and view Capitol Reef's world-class scenery and an even larger star-studded sky. Sometimes I feel great sadness, remembering warnings from a late U.S. senator from Utah on how best to preserve these and other enchanted lands.

The Milky Way over Capitol Reef National Park.
Credit: NPS/Jacob Frank

CHAPTER FOURTEEN
Diamonds in the Sky

"Art cannot replicate the natural world—neither the starry universe nor the voodoo gulches and hoodoo rocks of the canyon country, the high mesas, the sunken rivers, the corroded cliffs of the Colorado Plateau."

—EDWARD ABBEY

Utah Senator Frank E. "Ted" Moss was instrumental in setting aside national parks throughout the nation in what documentary filmmaker Ken Burns dubbed "America's best idea." Moss led the effort to set aside Capitol Reef as a national park in 1971. He also sponsored legislation protecting some of the Colorado Plateau's great wonders: Arches and Canyonlands National Parks, Flaming Gorge, Glen Canyon National Recreation Areas, and the Kolob Canyons expansion of the existing Zion National Park. He led the way in creating or expanding twelve other national parks, recreation areas, or protected national seashores and lakeshores in California, Indiana, Massachusetts, Michigan, New York, North Carolina, Oregon, Texas, Washington, D.C., Maryland, and Wisconsin.

Moss's work earned him the nickname "Mr. National Park."

Yet, he was forgotten by 1996 when President Bill Clinton, a fellow Democrat, set aside nearly two million acres of spectacular plateaus, mesas, buttes, slot canyons, and glorious views for the Grand Staircase-Escalante National Monument in Utah. Moss was not invited to the heavily hyped announcement made outside the state at the south rim of the Grand Canyon in neighboring Arizona. In fact, "Mr. National Park" was not even mentioned.

The snub, perhaps, serves as a metaphor for the precarious existence of national monuments.

Moss had warned that lands are best protected as national parks because the legislation carries with it the force of law. National monuments created by the stroke of a president's pen can be overturned when another administration comes into power. His words became prophetic in bitter struggles over presidents single-handedly declaring lands as monuments—or shrinking protected lands.

President Donald Trump proved Moss's point when he drastically downsized Utah's Grand Staircase, the size of Delaware with massive cliffs, called stairsteps, described by their colors for different epochs: chocolate (the oldest formation), vermillion, white, gray, and pink, as well as the Bears Ears National Monument, created by President Barack Obama.

President Joe Biden restored the monuments' original boundaries in 2021. But Utah leaders who remember Clinton's twenty-five-year-old insult by appearing in Arizona are fighting to overturn Biden's decision.[1]

Moss was defeated by Republican Orrin Hatch in 1976. During the campaign, Hatch repeatedly charged that Moss's three terms in the Senate were enough. Hatch, however, served seven terms before retiring in 2018. By the end of Hatch's tenure, Congress turned into a bitterly divided partisan body. The vitriol ended hopes that Congress would again set aside national parks with ironclad protections.

Capitol Reef is only a part of the massive red-rock country that lies

---

1. The *Deseret News* reminded readers of that long-ago slight, which "particularly charred Utah leaders' pride because Clinton made the announcement from the neighboring state of Arizona, without stepping foot on the land he was protecting."

within the Colorado Plateau. The Plateau's vast 130,000-square-mile landmass makes up much of Colorado, Utah, Arizona, and New Mexico. It is home to ten National Parks, twenty-one national monuments, and dozens of wilderness areas and state parks, giving it the greatest concentration of U.S. national parks and monuments outside Washington, D.C. Thirty-one Native American tribes claim the Colorado Plateau as their homeland, where reservations make up one-third of the landmass. Their contribution cannot be overstated in the history of this scenic landscape. As politicians debate development, Native Americans are calling for protections to be placed on their sacred places.

But the Plateau's value does not lie in just its landscape. Its large swatches of undeveloped land, arid climate, and high desert elevations make the Plateau one of the world's last dark sky regions. For generations, visitors have come to Utah's national parks to view world-class dreamlands, but now they also come to see the heavens.

"Many in the world have lost their view of the Milky Way," wrote David Mitchell and Terrell Gallaway in a study showing the economic benefits of star tourism. "For them a dark sky is as exotic a sight as a herd of bison or a glacial lake."

At my childhood home outside Los Angeles, there were days when the smog was so thick that my lungs ached whenever I took a deep breath. I rarely saw the night sky. My stepdad, Lyle Winder, was reared in Springdale, Utah, gateway to Zion National Park, and he often returned there, bringing our family along.[2]

Zion is where I first saw the Milky Way, glimpsing my tiny world's place in an incomprehensible, glittering universe.

But even around these parks, the sky is being blotted out by light

---

2. We camped at the foot of a 6,545-high mountain called the Watchman. This was my stepdad's ancestral home, which was taken over by the park. I marveled at the Great White Throne, a formation that has been called America's masterpiece. Today it is a symbol of the park.

pollution. One night, Torrey resident Mary Bedingfield-Smith, a retired Utah State University educator, noticed that a single streetlight near her home was so bright that it lit up a row of cottonwood trees, spoiling her view of Capitol Reef's star-encrusted sky. She met with town leaders with a proposal: Her group would raise money to install new lighting that would direct light beams downward instead of toward the night sky, and the municipality would save hundreds of dollars in lighting costs each year.

She assured residents that no one would be forced to replace existing lighting, and her group would pay new lighting costs for anyone who wanted to retrofit but couldn't afford it. In 2019, with bulb shields, directed lighting, and a dark-sky ordinance, Torrey became the first town in Utah—and the 18th in the world—to be named an International Dark Sky Community. It also was the first national park gateway community to achieve the designation.[3]

The Grand Canyon has also retrofitted its lights, making it one of the world's largest and most complex International Dark Sky Parks.

Visitors to the Morrill cabin have been awestruck when they've seen the stars and constellations for the first time. One woman asked how she would recognize the Milky Way. "You won't be able to miss it. You'll know," I answered as I gestured overhead, sweeping my arm from one horizon to the other.

Among other passersby who stop are relatives reared by the last woman to live in the cabin before I purchased the lot. Dicey Chesnut was the cabin's last pioneer.

---

3. I interviewed a county commissioner who was against retrofitting lighting because he felt the government would overreach its authority by telling homeowners and businesses what to do. He said his own city would not retrofit its street lighting on the theory that it would be a first step in government lighting mandates. "It's a slippery slope," he said.

Dicey Chesnut

CHAPTER FIFTEEN
Closing of the Frontier

"The Chesnutts (sic) were living folklore, survivors of the frontier. I would go a good way to have one of Mother Chesnutt's breakfasts again, with peaches and cream, hot biscuits, corned elk and eggs baked in the oven in a muffin tin."

—WALLACE STEGNER
American Places

Dicey Ann Staley Chesnut was the last person to live in the Morrill cabin until I bought it. And it was a long path that brought her here.

Early 20th-century historian Frederick Jackson Turner wrote that the frontier experience was the single most important influence on American life and culture. In 1890, however, the director of the U.S. Census Bureau announced that the frontier line—where the population density was less than two persons per square mile—no longer existed.[1] The frontier era had ended. The Chesnut family was part of that era, traveling long distances in horse-drawn wagons and laboring mightily to live off the land without relying on corporations, railroads, or banks.

The Chesnut family in America started with Annie Petersen, who

---

1. John Mack Faragher, *Rereading Frederick Jackson Turner*, 53.

converted to Mormonism in the town of Lindebjerg, Denmark. She accepted a marriage proposal, as a polygamous second wife, from Merritt Staley, who sent money to her for her passage over. He was forty-nine; she was twenty-two—younger than his two daughters. Though she spoke no English, Annie was the first in her family to sail from Denmark to the New World. She traveled alone on the voyage and boarded a transcontinental train to southern Utah. Merritt met her at the station and immediately took her to the Mexican state of Chihuahua, where they settled in Colonia Dublan. The colony was founded by Miles Park Romney (American politician Mitt Romney's great-grandfather)[2] in 1885 with his four wives and thirty children. In the U.S., the federal government had confiscated his property, stripped him of his voting rights, and jailed him for unlawful cohabitation, so the family fled to the Chihuahua desert.

Annie moved in with her husband's first family, her own family growing quickly until 1895 when Merritt died. Annie was pregnant with her fifth child. The family struggled. Annie gleaned grains from fields, took in washing, and worked in a store to feed her children. The shopkeeper took pity on the young widow and allowed her children to collect overripe fruit and siftings of sugar and flour left at the bottom of sacks. At times, the family had only cornbread and gravy to eat, and sometimes only gravy.

Two years after Merritt's death, Annie married a poor Danish immigrant, Jorgen Jorgensen, a widower with two young sons. He had a penchant for moving on when his luck ran out, which his chil-

---

2. George Romney, Miles Park's grandson, became chairman of American Motors Corp. He was also a three-term Michigan governor and presidential candidate, though he lost the 1968 Republican nomination to Richard Nixon when his Mormon faith was not widely understood. Mitt Romney, George's son, did get the Republican nomination for president, but lost to Barack Obama. He later became a U.S. senator for Utah.

dren called "moving fever." The new nine-person family moved into a renovated cowshed and five more children followed while they lived in Old Mexico.

The Jorgensen family fled the country during the hostilities that led up to the 1911 Mexican Revolution, though three of the siblings, now adults, opted to stay in Mexico. One of Annie's children, twenty-year-old Dicey,[3] who would someday live in my cabin, had recently married William Chesnut, and the new couple—along with William's mother—joined the travelers.

William, who was twenty-one when he married Dicey, was his mother's only child. He had bounced around settlements in the Utah Territory and Old Mexico as a boy due to his parents' polygamous entanglements. William's mother, Grace Knox, was his father's second wife—his first wife was her sister, who had died. William's father would go on to marry his own two young stepdaughters. William's parents divorced when he was a baby, but he had six surviving half-siblings and many cousins from his father's other three wives. (William himself married only one woman—Dicey.)

William learned the orchardist trade from his stepfather. But in 1894 his stepfather was killed when a horse reared up and kicked him in the stomach. William's widowed mother took him to Chihuahua, where she briefly remarried his biological father. But now she had decided to follow William and Dicey on their exodus from Old Mexico. The refugees in the party numbered three women, two men, and six children.

The families packed what they could onto two wagons and six horses and spent their first night in an open cave, hiding from bandits. They traveled for five days at a time during their journey, stopping on Saturdays and Sundays to give their teams a rest. Sometimes they paused longer, allowing foals to gain enough strength to keep up with

---

3. Born September 10, 1891, in Colonia Dublan.

the teams. They hauled water in barrels over the desert and pushed their wagons uphill in mountainous terrain, sometimes hitching all their horses to pull a single wagon. The men chained the wagons' back wheels on the downslopes and dragged a large tree trunk behind to slow their descent. The women washed and mended clothes and cooked bread over a campfire.

Dicey's half-brother, Ephraim Jorgensen, who was ten years old at the time, remembered the trek as a sort of game. He rode his pretty palomino alongside the wagons and sometimes dashed into camp unexpectedly to surprise the grownups. He described his horse as a friend, always knowing "what I wanted her to do." But when the families reached Deming, New Mexico, less than forty miles north of the Mexican border, they ran out of money. The refugees had hundreds of miles to go.

"Something had to be done and my horse was the only thing that could be sold and of course that is what was done," Ephraim wrote years later. "I think part of me stayed there and life was not the same anymore."

After sixty days on the trail, the arduous nine-hundred-mile journey from Chihuahua through New Mexico, Arizona, and Colorado, finally brought the family to Ferron, Utah. The horses were worn out and could go no farther. William and Dicey Chesnut continued on to join some relatives in the desert outpost of Escalante. In a photograph taken around 1917 when she was thirty years old, Dicey appears to be the older sister of her two children rather than their mother. Dicey had a clear, kind, finely cut Scandinavian countenance that belied her years of arduous labor.

In Escalante, they were reunited with their friend Henry Heaps who was mourning the loss of his twelve-year-old son, who had died from a weak heart. Only a few months later, in 1919, his wife died in childbirth, leaving him alone to care for nine children. Henry named the baby after his late wife, Eliza Alice, and entrusted her to the Chesnuts.

The Chesnuts finally settled in Fruita at the confluence of Sulphur Creek and the Fremont River, nicknamed the Dirty Devil for its frequent floods.[4] Twelve people lived in the two-story home they built: Dicey and William, the daughter they had adopted, their own four children, and William's widowed brother and his four children, whom Dicey mothered. Fruita bestowed bounties not seen in the surrounding desert landscape. The Chesnut's orchard of peaches, apples, berries, and almonds was sheltered by towering cliffs close enough that it seemed Dicey could touch them from her front porch. The family picked fruit, tended a garden, and raised livestock. After President Franklin Roosevelt declared Capitol Reef a national monument in 1937, the Chesnuts built two cabins and enclosed a side porch at their own home to accommodate tourists, whom Dicey cooked for. They also installed a small hand-cranked gas pump.

Author Wallace Stegner, who stopped at one of the cabins, said the old days "were sort of wrapped up in the Chesnutt (*sic*) place." The buildings were torn down after the Park Service took over their homestead. "Capitol Reef would be richer if the Chesnutt store had been kept," he wrote. "The land is not complete without its human history and associations. Scenery by itself is pretty sterile. The Chesnutts were living folklore, survivors of the frontier."[5]

It was inevitable that many would sell their property to the Park Service. The small valley never supported more than ten families, with frequent flooding along the Fremont River that wiped out crops and washed out the dirt roads. Dicey's granddaughter, Ellen Chesnut Rawlings, wrote that the road to Fruita was so treacherous she feared her

---

4. Today their old homestead is the picnic area and a campground at Capitol Reef National Park. Visitors pick from the fruit trees that William Chesnut and other settlers had planted.

5. Wallace Stegner, *American Places* (New Jersey: Wing Books, 1993), 124.

sweetheart would stop making the drive to visit her. "It was just a dirt road, graded when possible, winding down the steep twisting cliffs and dugways through Sulphur Creek," she wrote. "Travel on it was time consuming and troublesome. The first time Bill, my husband-to-be, drove down to see me, he found himself with a flat tire and a broken oil line."

Dicey's son Clarence brought his bride to live with his parents in Fruita. Dicey and her daughter-in-law Ruby became lifelong friends. After Dicey's husband died of cancer in 1948, she could not stay in Fruita. Others in her household had already left after the small school-house closed in 1941.[6] Dicey did not want to leave her home in this picturesque hamlet that Wallace Stegner described as "a sudden in-tensely green little valley among the cliffs of the Water-pocket Fold, op-ulent with cherries, peaches and apples." But Fruita was dying and too isolated for an elderly woman to live alone. Her son had built a home for his family in Torrey, and next-door Clarence added a third room to the Morrill cabin for Dicey. For the first time, the old house had indoor plumbing, a kitchen, and a bathroom. When Dicey relocated there in the early 1950s, she became the last pioneer to live in the board cabin built by Torrey town founder George Morrill in 1886. It is the only original home still standing.

In her old age, Dicey enjoyed an extensive family. She and her daughter-in-law, who lived next door, often spent afternoons together. Dicey never lost contact with her foster daughter, whom her children called their sister, or the four nephews and nieces she had cared for. Many of them had large families of their own, giving Dicey, nicknamed

---

6. Today the log school is a roadside attraction. Fruita's first teacher was a twelve-year-old girl. Nettie Behunin taught twenty-two students, three of whom were her siblings. When the school opened in 1896, only eight families—with numerous chil-dren—lived in the town. The school closed when there were not enough students to keep it open.

Grandma Great, a broad and grand legacy.

The beloved Dicey gave her grandchildren a taste of frontier life. They helped her make soap from lard and lye, a mixture of ashes soaked in water and boiled in a cauldron over a campfire. They picked peaches from the family's five hundred trees in Fruita and helped harvest a large garden. The family would often crowd together for a hot midday dinner of pork, beef, or wild game, pickled vegetables, homemade biscuits, jam, and fruit cobbler.

An orchard in Fruita, Utah. Credit: NPS/Jacob Frank.

Dicey was a first cousin to Mark E. Petersen, an apostle in the Mormon Church's highest governing body from 1944 until his death in 1984. Family members say Dicey Chesnut loved listening to his sermons on an old radio during church conferences, which were broadcast worldwide. Though the family was large, Mark never forgot Dicey. He spoke at her funeral in 1974. She was the last of a generation of pioneers.

After Dicey's death, the Morrill cabin was boarded up for forty years until 2013. That was when I bought it and started on my journey to discover some of its stories. I am reminded of a passage from Gladys Taber's *Stillmeadow Daybook*, an account of rural life in a 17th-century Connecticut farmhouse the author had restored: "Old houses, I thought, do not belong to people ever, not really, people belong to them." I would add that old houses reveal fragments of a forgotten past—and show our connections to diverse people and communities we never knew existed. I came to understand over ten years of restoring and researching the cabin that I, too, had traveled the trail to Poverty Flat.

Ethalinda Jane Young Morrill and George Drury Morrill
Credit: Gloria Miller Allen.

APPENDIX
Pioneer Recipes and Remedies

It's possible to get a glimpse into Ethalinda's kitchen by perusing recipes published in century-old Utah newspapers. The Morrill cabin was never large enough for a kitchen. Even after George built an addition, only a corner of the original room was set aside for cooking. A fireplace and later a wood furnace provided the heat for cooking.

Ethalinda waited years for their orchard to produce, and nearly fifteen years after moving into the cabin, she bartered for bottles so she could can her own fresh fruit.

Squash, root vegetables, and fruit preserves were stored in an outside cellar. Potatoes were buried in the cellar's dirt floor. Meat was dried or dangled from a rope in a dry well. Water came from barrels, a cistern, and later a spigot in the back room. Ethalinda filtered the water to remove pollywogs, specks of dirt, and mud.

These newspaper recepies show that food preparation was time-consuming and sometimes toxic. One recipe calls for whipping egg whites to seal preserves. Others describe pounding biscuit dough with an ax handle for a half hour or fermenting tomatoes into wine. Remedies were unreliable and often dangerous. Buttermilk was supposed to cure cholera, garlic dissolved in whiskey was supposed to kill intestinal worms, and a silk handkerchief could mend a broken leg—given enough time.

These concoctions shouldn't be tried, only enjoyed as a time capsule of the old frontier.

FOOD

Buckwheat Cakes

To one pint of buckwheat flour, while dry, add two teaspoonfuls Royal Baking Powder, a teaspoonful salt, one scant tablespoonful brown sugar or New Orleans molasses to make them brown, mix well together, and when ready to bake, add one pint cold water, or sufficient to form a batter, stir but little and bake immediately on a hot griddle.

—*Deseret News,* Dec. 14, 1881

Good Biscuits

Rub a quarter pound of butter, sweet and fresh, into three pounds of flour, use as little cold water in mixing it as possible, for the dough must be exceedingly stiff, as stiff as it can possibly be worked. When thoroughly kneaded pound it with a wooden mallet or an axe, rolling it up whenever pounded flat. Continue pounding for half an hour, or until the dough is as smooth as putty, then break off small bits and work into cakes the size of a dollar, in thickness a quarter inch. Bake from half to three quarters of an hour. The biscuit must be thinner in the center than at the edges, and must be pricked with a fork.

—*Deseret News,* Oct 29, 1856

Fry Chicken

The chickens are killed, scalded, picked and washed out cleanly in water, then quartered and thrown into boiling butter. In a few minutes they are done brown, and are then to be removed and served up hot and dry, not put into grease again.

—*Woman's Exponent*, Feb. 15, 1875

Potato Salad

Eggs, two yolks; sugar, one teaspoonful; butter, a piece the size of a hen's egg. Beat the yolks, mix with the other ingredients and boil, stirring constantly, until pretty thick. Slice boiled potatoes into a salad dish, and pour the dressing over just before sending to the table.

—*Salt Lake Herald-Republican*, April 28, 1877

Tomato Catsup

Take one bushel of tomatoes, and boil them until they are soft — squeeze them through a fine wire sieve, and add half a gallon of vinegar; three half-pints of salt, two ounces of cloves, quarter of a pound of allspice, three ounces of cayenne pepper, three table spoonful of black pepper, and five heads of garlic, skinned and separated. Mix together, and boil about three hours, or until reduced to about one half, then bottle without straining.

—*Deseret News*, Aug. 27, 1856

Pickled Cantaloupes

Take the cantaloupes or musk-melons [cut] in the cores lengthwise; peel and lay in a stone jar; cover with good cider vinegar, and let stand twenty four hours; then take out; measure the vinegar, less than three pints or two quarts — all of it makes too much syrup; to every quart of vinegar, three pounds of brown sugar, half an ounce each of cloves, cinnamon, and mace, whole; boil all together util the melon is clear and easily penetrated with a silver fork; take out and lay in your jar; boil the syrup fifteen minutes longer, and pour over the melon while hot.

—*Salt Lake Herald-Republican,* Sept. 23, 1877

Tomato Wine

Express the juice of ripe tomatoes, put one pound of sugar to each quart of juice and bottle. In a few weeks it will have the appearance and flavor of pure wine of the best kind. No alcohol is needed to preserve it. Mixed with water it is a delightful beverage for the sick.

—*Union Vedette,* Oct. 18, 1867

Tomato Jam

Quarter some good ripe tomatoes like an orange and remove the core; allow one pound of sugar to each pound of fruit and boil it till it sets, when it is papered down like any other jam. Another way is to scald the tomatoes, peel them and press the pulp through a sieve, finishing off as above. If the fruit is quartered and put on over the fire the juice can then be run out and finished off like ordinary jelly.

—*Salt Lake Times,* Aug 21, 1890

Egg Lemonade

Break an egg into a tumbler; rub two lumps of sugar on the rind of a fine lemon; put the sugar into the tumbler; squeeze the lemon into it and half fill the tumbler with ice broken small; fill up with water and with a shaker shake the whole vigorously for a few seconds: then grate a little nutmeg over the top. If you have no shaker beat the egg with a fork.

—*Salt Lake Herald-Republican,* Oct. 18, 1890

Fruit Pies

No undercrust should be made to apple or any fruit pie. It is always heavy and not fit to eat. Place a narrow rim of paste around the edge of the plate, and fill with the fruit either raw or stewed, and cover it. The juices will be retained much better, and it will see a sight of butter and flour, which is no trifling consideration in these days.

—*Deseret News,* Aug. 20, 1856

Preserves

Apply the white of an egg, with a suitable brush, to a single thickness of white tissue paper, with which cover the jars, overlapping the edges an inch or two. When dry, the whole will become as tight as a drum. Those who have not Arthur's patent jars, may follow this mode.

—*Deseret News,* Aug. 20, 1856

Sealing Wax

A very good sealing wax [for fruit cans] is made by melting and stirring well together one ounce of Venice turpentine, four ounces of common rosin, and six ounces of gum shellac. A beautiful red color may be given by adding one-quarter of an ounce or less of vermillion.

—*Deseret News,* July 15, 1857

Vinegar

Put two quarts of corn meal in a bag and place it in a tub, pour into the bag six quarts of boiling water and let it remain two or three days, then press the water from the bag into that in the tub or vessel in which you wish to make your vinegar. In about three or four weeks you will have vinegar quite equal to cider vinegar.

—*Deseret News,* July 22, 1857

Rhubarb Vinegar

Take 25 ordinary sized stalks of rhubarb; pound or crush them with a piece of wood in the bottom of a strong tub; add 10 gallons of water; let this stand 24 hours; strain off the crushed rhubarb, add 18 pounds of sugar free from molasses, and a teacupful of the best brewer's yeast; raise the temperature to 65 or 68 degrees, and put your browst into a 11-gallon cask; place it in a position where the temperature will not fall below 60 degrees. In a month strain off from the grounds, returning it to the cask again, and let it stand till it becomes vinegar.

—*Salt Lake Herald-Republican,* July 3, 1870

Substitute for Coffee

To one quart of wheat bran add one teacupful of molasses with one of water, stir together and dry in the shade; or in a stove; brown a dark color and mix one-third coffee, which, if prepared right, makes an excellent beverage.

—*Deseret News,* April 6, 1864

Coffee

Prepare two coarse or white flannel bags, put in each the required quantity of coffee, boil one bag and contents until the strength is extracted, then remove the bag and put in the fresh one. Let this steep or simmer without boiling. The first portion supplies the strength, the latter, the aroma and as the strength still remains in this portion, it may be boiled for the next coffee required.

—*The Salt Lake Tribune,* Nov. 15, 1879

Brine

Pack your beef close into the barrel, then take three ounces of saltpeter, ten pounds of salt and twelve quarts of water, for every one hundred pounds of beef. Put these into your kettle and boil until well dissolved. Then pour on boiling hot upon the beef, cover the barrel close to keep in the stream.

—*Deseret News,* Jan. 1, 1862

Saving Flour

Knead your bread in the bowl till it will no longer adhere to your hands, then dip your hands in the flour and rub off all the dough that clings to them. Sprinkle very little flour on the board, taking care not to scatter it but keep it only where it will be needed. [Put] a little flour in the bowl and, with it, rub off all the dough that remains, and work it in with the bread. Scrape off all the flour and such dough as may stick to the moulding board, which should be very little. Put what is thus scraped up in the bottom of the bread bowl, and when the dough is raised enough to go into the pans this flour at the bottom of the bowl will be light enough to work into the dough and thus be saved.

—*Salt Lake Herald-Republican,* Jan. 17, 1879

Bread

One cup Indian meal, one graham flour, one sour milk, one warm water and one-half cup of molasses; add one teaspoon soda and salt to taste. Steam three hours and then dry in oven.

—*Salt Lake Herald-Republican,* Nov. 7, 1896

Potato Yeast

Pare, boil and mash smooth twelve potatoes; stir into these one large cup of sugar, and one quart of boiling water; when cool, add one quart of cold water, and a half pint or less of yeast; keep it in a warm place for twelve hours, when it will be ready for use. Shake it carefully before using; always reserve a small quantity of old yeast for raising the new.

—*Deseret News,* June 25, 1856

Brown Bread

Take flour made of good wheat, ground down without bolting; use good yeast only for raising; make up and bake as every good breadmaker does with fine flour. It is better to bake in a moderate heat and rather longer than required for fine flour. By adding about a tablespoonful of good molasses (when kneading) for every ordinary sized loaf, the bread will retain its moisture and softness till several days or a week old.

—*Deseret News,* Jan. 19, 1857

Cupcakes

Three cups of flour, one cup of butter, two cups of brown sugar, one cup of stoned raisins or English currants, one cup of wine or cider, two tablespoonfuls of cream or melted pork drip, one teaspoonful of soda. Season with nutmeg or cinnamon. Bake in small tins.

—*Salt Lake Herald-Republican,* May 26, 1889

Ice Cream

Beat the yolks of four eggs until lemon-colored and thick; add one pound of powdered sugar and a quart of milk just brought to the boiling point; cook two minutes - no longer. Stir in the whites of four eggs well beaten, a teaspoonful and a half of vanilla and a half teaspoonful of almond. When cool add one quart of cream and freeze.

—*Deseret Weekly,* Oct. 16, 1897

Taffy

Either of the two kinds of molasses candy, if poured from the kettle into tan trays without working, will produce a fine plain taffy. It may be left inside of the tray or when slightly cold may be marked off into squares.

—*Utah Journal,* May 29, 1883

Tutti-frutti

Begin by putting one pound each of sugar and hulled strawberries in a covered stone jar, with one quart of good brandy or whisky. If high flavor is wanted, add a little pounded mace and grated lemon peel or a race of ginger, well bruised. Let stand until cherries come, then put in a pound of them, one-half seeded, the rest with the pits, along with a second pound of sugar. In like manner add plums, raspberries, peaches, pears and grapes, as they come in season, putting in with each sort of fruit its allotted pound of sugar, and now and then a little more spice.

—*Salt Lake Herald-Republican,* April 30, 1899

AILMENTS

Silk Kerchiefs

Sore throats vanish when encircled in a silken kerchief. [The] grand-mothers knew all about it a hundred years ago. They believed too that silk would cure all other diseases, and some of them thought it would heal a broken leg, "if only taken in time." We do not go as far as that, but we know that silk will absorb electricity as readily as a Leyden jar.

—*The Salt Lake Tribune,* Feb. 4, 1883

Drunkenness

Sulphate of iron 5 grains; magnesia, 10 grains; peppermint water, 11 drachms; spirit of nutmeg, 1 drachm; take twice a day. Where the appetite for liquor is not very strong, the medicine at once supplies the place of the accustomed drams; their amount should be decreased gradually, until the desire for them entirely ceases.

—*Deseret News,* May 1, 1861

Putrid Sore Throat

A poultice made of the yolk of an egg and fine salt, of a paste like con-sistency, to be put on the throat, and kept on 30 minutes, unless sooner dry. {A} wash or gargle should also be prepared and used, consisting of equal parts of fine salt and alum, mixed with vinegar.

—*Deseret News,* Oct. 19, 1864

Colds

It is an erroneous notion that bathing renders a person more liable to "take cold by opening the pores." Colds are produced by disturbance of the circulation, not by opening or closing of the pores of the skin. Frequent bathing increases the activity of the circulation in the skin so that a person is far less subject to chilliness and to take cold.

—*Deseret News,* Nov. 17, 1886

Worms

Irish Remedy: Garlic dissolved in good whisky and kept in a bottle for use, it is said to be a sovereign remedy for worms. Dose from a tea-spoonful to a tablespoonful every morning.

—*Deseret News,* Jan. 11, 1855

Rheumatism

The cure of stiff joints from the effects of rheumatism - Beat quite thin the yolk of a new laid egg and add by degrees, three ounces of water; shake it well, that the egg and water may be well mixed. This is to be applied to the contracted parts, either cold or milk warm, rubbing it well three or four times a day.

—*Deseret News,* Oct. 29, 1856

Cholera

New buttermilk and sweet milk, equal parts boiled together and strained, and taken inwardly by the sufferer.

—*Salt Lake Herald-Republican*, Aug. 20, 1875

Small Pox

Sulphate of zinc, one grain, fox glove, (Digitalis,) one grain, half a teaspoon twice full of water; when thoroughly mixed add four ounces of water. Take a spoonful every hour.

—*Salt Lake Herald-Republican*, July 29, 1871

Cough

Take of boneset (plant) as much as you can grasp in your hand, and two quarts of water; boil it to one quart; add a pint of molasses; let it simmer a few minutes, and then strain and set it by to cool. Take one gill (teacup) three times a day before eating; it is an excellent remedy.

—*Deseret News*, July 12, 1850

Whooping Cough

Butter, 1oz.; vinegar, 6 tablespoonsful; honey, 4 tablespoonsful; half a nutmeg, grated, and a sprinkling of red pepper. Simmer slowly in a covered vessel. A dose, a tablespoonful, and should be taken at short intervals.

—*Salt Lake Herald-Republican*, Feb. 7, 1875

Consumption

Put a dozen whole lemons in cold water and boil until soft (not too soft), roll and squeeze until the juice is all extracted. Should they cause pain or looseness of the bowels, lessen the quantity and use five or six a day until better, then begin and use a dozen again.

—*Deseret News,* Aug. 22, 1877

Diphtheria

1/2 Pint Alcohol: 1 Tablespoonful Chlorate Potash, Saltpetre and Sulphor: 1 Teaspoonful burnt Borax. Put in a bottle with half pint of water, and shake well before using. Dose for an adult, one teaspoonful every two hours till relieved. If severe, every half hour for a while. For small children reduce it a little.

—*Southern Utonian,* Jan. 21, 1887

The Morrill Cabin. Credit: Gloria Miller Allen.

HOME

Hair

Soft, natural-looking waves of hair are made by rolling the hair over large soft papers or kid curlers, rolling from the top of the curl toward the end. The hair should be wet and left in the rolls over night. If this is not done, pinch the curls with a hot iron. If you wish to have the hair set out around the face, turn the teeth of your side combs toward the face, not away from it. Catch them through the end of your waves and you can "fluff" the hair as little or as much as you choose.

—*The Salt Lake Tribune,* Sept. 8, 1895

Lotion

Take one pint of alcohol and two ounces of castor oil, and shake them together for fifteen minutes in a bottle. It will then be found that the alcohol has dissolved the oil, and the combination of the two makes a very excellent lotion for the hair. It can be perfumed with a few drops of the essential oils.

—*Deseret News,* Dec. 29, 1858

Brows

First brush your brows towards your nose, then take your pencil and rub lightly through the hairs. When you must use your first finger and thumb, which you may moisten slightly, pinch the hairs into a narrow and prettily curved line above the eyes.

—*Salt Lake Times,* May 19, 1890

Scented Water

Take one ounce of essential oil of lavender, one and a half pints of spirits of wine, and one drop of musk. Put all these into a quart bottle and shake this mixture well for some time. Then leave it to settle for a few days, when it must be shaken again. It should then be poured into small bottles, which should be hermetically sealed.

—*Salt Lake Herald-Republican,* Oct. 3, 1896

Shoe Shine

Orange juice is one of the best dressings for black shoes or boots. Take a slice or quarter of an orange and rub it on the shoe or boot; then, when dry brush with a soft brush until the shoe shines like a looking glass.

—*Deseret Evening News,* March 8, 1898

Soap

Save the lye of sufficient strength to float an egg; measure it into barrels as obtained, and to each gallon add one pound of grease. Stir every day till it becomes thick; then to sixteen gallons of this soft soap put four gallons of lye, as strong as that above. Boil one hour or more, till the grease entirely disappears; then dissolve six quarts of salt in four gallons of water; stir it in and boil the whole fifteen minutes longer; pour it into the tubs to harden; cut it out in bars, and dry in the shade.

—*Deseret News,* Feb. 27, 1856

Cheap Candles

To twelve pounds of lard use alum and salt-peter each one pound; dissolve the alum and salt-peter in a small quantity of water, then pour into the melted lard, and boil the whole until the water evaporates. The mixture requires constant stirring to prevent settling in the bottom of the vessel. Candles made of this composition are equal to the best tallow, and last some time longer.

—*Deseret News,* Jan. 25, 1855

Glue Polished Steel

Dissolve five or six bits of gum mastic, each the size of a large pea, in as much spirits of wine as will suffice to render it liquid. In another vessel, dissolve in brandy as much isinglass, previously softened in water, as will make a two ounce vial of strong glue, adding two small bits of gum ammonia, which must be rubbed until dissolved. Then mix the whole heat. Keep in a vial closely stopped. When it is to be used, set the vial in boiling water.

—*Salt Lake Herald-Republican,* Oct. 21, 1870

Flatware Repair

An exchange says, that if you wish to refasten the loose handles of knives and forks, make your cement of common brick-dust and rosin melted together. Seal engravers understand this recipe.

—*Deseret News,* Dec. 11, 1852

Laundry

To every pound of soap add from one-half to three quarters of an ounce of common borax, with one quart of water. Put the water in any convenient vessel upon the stove, add the borax, somewhat pulverized, and then put in the soap cut up in thin pieces. Keep them hot, but not boiling for two or three hours, or until the whole is dissolved, and then set aside to cool, when a solid mass will be formed. If the vessel is set upon the warm stove at night, the operation will be completed in the morning, tho' we think it better to stir the mass just before it is cooled.

—*Deseret News,* Oct. 17, 1855

Copper

A copper boiler or tea kettle may be kept clean by a daily washing in buttermilk, rubbing dry with a flannel. Fresh milk may be used, but buttermilk is better.

—*Salt Lake Herald-Republican,* Jan. 17, 1879

Oilcloth Restorer

Melt one-half of an ounce of beeswax in a saucer of turpentine. Rub the surface of the oilcloth all over with the mixture, and then rub it with a dry cloth.

—*Salt Lake Herald-Republican,* July 16, 1889

Table Settings

No dining table is considered properly dressed without the heavy silence cloth of felt or canton flannel placed under the tablecloth to give it body and deaden the sound.

—*Deseret Weekly,* May 15, 1897

Zinc Bath Tubs

A little kerosene is an excellent thing for cleansing a zinc bath tub. Apply with a soft woolen cloth then wash off with hot water—no soap in it—and polish with a powdered bath brick.

—*Salt Lake Herald-Republican,* May 23, 1896

Stepping Stones

The stones of a yard and doorsteps frequently have a greenish look which is very unsightly. In order to remove this, wash the stones with the following preparation: Half a pound of soda and a quarter of a pound of chloride of lime in a quart of boiling water. The greenness will steadily disappear.

—*Salt Lake Herald-Republican,* Nov. 15, 1896

Credit: Maura Naughton.

BIBLIOGRAPHY

Bagley, Will. *Blood of the Prophets: Brigham Young and the Massacre at Mountain Meadows.* Norman: University of Oklahoma Press, 2002.

Behunin, Cleo Teeples. "Life Story of Ethalinda Jane Morrill." In the author's possession.

Betenson, W.J. "Bill". *Butch Cassidy, My Uncle.* Glendo, WY: High Plains Press, 2012.

Bigler, David L., and Will Bagley. *The Mormon Rebellion, America's First Civil War, 1857–1858.* Norman: University of Oklahoma Press, 2011.

Bradshaw, Hazel, and Nellie Jenson. *Under Dixie Sun, A History of Washington County by Those Who Loved Their Forebears.* N.p.: Washington County Chapter D.U.P., 1950.

Brooks, Juanita. *The Mountain Meadows Massacre.* Norman: University of Oklahoma Press, 1962.

Brooks, Juanita, and Robert Glass Cleland, eds. *A Mormon Chronicle: The Diaries of John D. Lee 1848–1876.* 2 vols. Salt Lake City: University of Utah Press, 1983.

Carter, Thomas, and Peter Goss. *Utah's Historic Architecture: A Guide 1847–1940.* Salt Lake City: Utah State Historical Society, 1988.

Clarke, Joy, and Sherry M. Smith. "Life Sketch of George Drury Morrill." Pioneer History Files. International Society Daughters of Utah Pioneers, Salt Lake City.

Clarke, Joy Huntsman. "My Grandmother—Ethalinda Jane Young

Morrill. In the author's possession.

Davidson, George E. *Red Rock Eden, The Story of Fruita, One of Mormon Country's Most Isolated Settlements.* Torrey, UT: Capitol Reef National History Association, 1986.

Eckersley, Joseph. Diary. Joseph Eckersley Papers 1866–1960. LDS Church Archives. Salt Lake City: The Church of Jesus Christ of Latter-day Saints.

Faragher, John Mack, ed. *Rereading Frederick Jackson Turner: The significance of the Frontier in American History and Other Essays.* New York: Henry Holt & Co, 1994.

Gibbs, J.F. *Lights and Shadows of Mormonism.* Salt Lake City: Salt Lake Tribune Publishing Co., 1909.

Harvey, Thomas J. *Rainbow Bridge to Monument Valley: Making the Modern Old West.* Norman: University of Oklahoma Press, 2001.

Hobbs, George B. "First Exploration of the Forbidding San Juan." *Deseret Semi-Weekly News*, Dec. 29, 1919.

Hunter, Milton R. *Utah: The Story of Her People, 1540–1947: A Centennial History of Utah.* Salt Lake City: The Deseret News Press, 1946.

Huntsman, Myrtle. "The Life of Myrtle Violet Morrill Huntsman as told to her daughter, Joy H. Clarke, compiler." familysearch.org/tree/person/memories/KWZ3-F4T.

Hill, James B. "History of Utah State Prison 1850–1952." Master's thesis, Brigham Young University, 1952. scholarsarchive.byu.edu/etd/4791.

Jacobs, Mildred Hill. "History of John William Young, my great grandfather (1828–1891)." In *Pioneer History.* Salt Lake City: International Society Daughters of Utah Pioneers, 2006.

Kelly, Charles. *The Outlaw Trail, A History of Butch Cassidy and His Wild Bunch.* New York: Bonanza Books, 1959.

Kidd, James Harvey. Letters 1862–1865. Bentley Historical Library, University of Michigan. bentley.umich.edu.

Kimball, James. *J. Golden Kimball Stories: Mormonism's Colorful Cowboy*. Salt Lake City: Whitehorse Books, 1999.

Kimball, Monique Elaine. "A Matter of Faith: A Study of the Muddy Mission." Master's thesis, University of Nevada, Las Vegas, 1988.

Lee, Coral Coffey. *Index and Companion Book to Our Beloved Torrey*. Self-published, 2014.

Malmquist, O.N. *The First 100 Years: A History of The Salt Lake Tribune 1871–1971*. Salt Lake City: Utah State Historical Society, 1971.

Michigan Genealogy on the Web. migenweb.org/michiganinthewar andusgenweb.org.

Maxwell, John Gary. *Gettysburg to Great Salt Lake: George R. Maxwell, Civil War Hero and Federal Marshal Among the Mormons*. Norman: University of Oklahoma Press, 2010.

Meadows, Anne. *Digging Up Butch and Sundance*. New York: St. Martin's Press, 1994.

Miller, David E. *Hole-in-the-Rock: An Epic in the Colonization of the Great American West*. Salt Lake City: University of Utah Press, 1966.

Murphy, Miriam B. *A History of Wayne County*. Salt Lake City: Utah State Historical Society, 1999.

Newell, Linda King. *A History of Piute County*. Salt Lake City: Utah State Historical Society, 1999.

Olson, Virgil J., and Helen Olson. *Capitol Reef: The Story Behind the Scenery*. Whittier, CA: KC Publications, Inc., 1972.

Perkins, Cornelia Adams, Marian Gardner Nielson, and Lenora Butt Jones. *Saga of San Juan*. N.p.: San Juan County Daughters of Utah Pioneers, 1957.

Reid, H. Lorenzo. *Dixie of the Desert*. Zion National Park, UT: Zion Natural History Association, 1964.

Roylance, Ward J. "An Introduction to the Park." In *The Capitol Reef Reader*, edited by Stephen Trimble. Salt Lake City: University of

Utah Press, 2019.

Sayward, Dorothy Steward. "Comfort Magazine, 1888–1942: A History and Critical Study." *University of Maine Bulletin* 62, no. 13 (Jan. 20, 1960).

Smith, Mary Ann Young. "Mary Ann Young Smith, granddaughter to John and Margaret Young, as told to her niece, Maurine Allred Murphy, 1970." In possession of the author.

Snow, Anne, comp. *Rainbow Views, A History of Wayne County.* Springville, UT: Art City Publishing Co., 1953.

Stegner, Wallace. *Mormon Country.* New York: Duell, Sloan & Pearce, 1942.

Stegner, Wallace, and Page Stegner. *American Places.* New York, E. P. Dutton, 1981.

Stinchfield, Rick. *Capitol Reef National Park: The Complete Hiking and Touring Guide.* Boulder, CO: Westcliffe Publishers, 2010.

Stokes, William Lee. *Geology of Utah.* Salt Lake City: Utah Museum of Natural History, 1989.

United States Department of Agriculture Census of Agriculture. Historical Archive. Albert R. Mann Library, Cornell University.

Walker, Ronald W., Richard E. Turley Jr., and Glen M. Leonard. *Massacre at Mountain Meadows.* New York: Oxford University Press, 2008.

ACKNOWELDGMENTS

A few years before his death in 1919, George Morrill received a church blessing that his many labors would someday become known to his neighbors. I like to think that the Morrill historian Sherry Smith is a fulfillment of the family prophecy. She has recorded countless memories, which would otherwise have been lost. I am indebted to her lifetime of work.

Family patriarch Vance Morrill provided encouragement and contacts to many other relatives. One night, my son Matt Tracy and I showed up late at his Flute Shop motel outside Torrey when most other rooms in surrounding towns had been rented. Vance brought us warm blankets, a heater, and refused payment. When I insisted, he told us to use the money to buy something nice for the cabin.

Coral Lee Coffey provided stories and gifted books she wrote on the Lee side of the family. She did not know until college about her ancestor's conviction in the horrific Mountain Meadows Massacre. She was warm and gracious, sharing whatever information I needed. We had long conversations about the town's history at her own historic home and she often gave me fruit and vegetables from her garden.

The late preeminent historian Will Bagley answered questions and encouraged me to keep writing, as did the kind, late Richard E. Turley Jr., a scholar for The Church of Jesus Christ of Latter-day Saints. Wayne County historian Steve Taylor opened his voluminous files, answered many questions, and became a valued friend.

Editor Stephen Carter was instrumental in helping me bridge the gap from writing as a journalist to becoming an author. He is talented, patient, and took the time to explain various narrative techniques.

Ann Poore, a *Tribune* colleague and friend, provided valuable insights gleaned from her years as an acclaimed writer and art critic.

Maura Naughton, an accomplished watercolorist, gave critical suggestions on artwork for the book and contributed her own creations as well.

Others contributing artwork include Gloria Miller Allen, a teacher, author, and painter; and Steve Jorgensen, an award-winning, multi-disciplined artist.

I became friends with Ken Baxter and his wife after the couple sold me his painting of the Morrill cabin that appears on the book cover. They reduced the price and took whatever payment I could afford— which wasn't much at the time.

My daughters Sarah Gardiner and Rachel Davies cleared my painting debt as a Christmas present.

My son Matt did much of the restoration work when contractors refused to bid on a falling-down 19th-century shack. He also did the architectural drawings for the few contractors who took a chance to work on the long-abandoned house.

My daughter Elizabeth Volmer, a gifted educator, taught me advanced computer skills, spending hours patiently explaining steps she had already taught me more than once before.

Ben Rolly, my stepson and an accomplished actor, has produced and narrated an audio version of this book.

My brother Tom House lent me money when my funds dried up. Tom became my on-call expert, helping me become somewhat proficient in living in a rural community and doing maintenance work on an old home. During one stormy day, he brought his tractor to dig trenches to get water, which had been turned off for more than a half-century, to save trees in shock from lack of water. I have always turned to him whenever I get in a jam. My brother Fred's widow, Ann House, walked with me through his death to ensure those painful memories were accurately recounted. She also comforted me when my own sister died. When I told her that my sister and I had always planned on being crazy old ladies together, she asked, "Will I do instead?" Yes. You've done nicely.

I must honor my late stepfather, Lyle Winder, who took us from our home outside Los Angeles on numerous visits to his childhood community in Springdale, the gateway town to Zion National Park. He introduced me to the generosity of struggling rural families and neighbors. Our love for him is etched on his tombstone. It reads Beloved Stepfather.

My husband, newspaper columnist Paul Rolly, did not share my dream of restoring the cabin but supported me in every way possible. He spent hours running errands, making suggestions on the manuscript, and editing my work, even though I knew he was happy simply attending our grandkids' sporting events.

I did not write this book alone. I am grateful for the help in writing about forgotten stories I found charming, haunting, and inspiring.

INDEX

DAWN HOUSE

Dawn House is a 35-year newspaper veteran. *The Salt Lake Tribune* nominated her for the Pulitzer Prize after she tracked down historic LDS documents tied to a forgery scam and murder investigation. Her research documents, the Dawn House Papers, are stored in Special Collections at the University of Utah. She earned a bachelor's degree in English and history from Brigham Young University. She completed coursework in the University of Utah's communications graduate program and taught as an adjunct professor there. She was Journalist-in-Residence at Utah State University. *Photo Credit: Scott T. Smith*

Made in the USA
Monee, IL
07 June 2023

35317389R00115